Hands On or Hands Off?

Hong Kong University Press thanks Xu Bing for writing the Press's name in his Square Word Calligraphy for the covers of its books. For further information, see p. iv.

Hands On or Hands Off?
The Nature and Process of Economic Policy in Hong Kong

Tony Latter

香港大學出版社
HONG KONG UNIVERSITY PRESS

Hong Kong University Press
14/F Hing Wai Centre
7 Tin Wan Praya Road
Aberdeen
Hong Kong

© Hong Kong University Press 2007

Hardback   ISBN 978-962-209-860-2
Paperback ISBN 978-962-209-861-9

Cover illustrations on the paperback edition:

"COSCO HIT container port/terminal." Copyright © 2003 Hong Kong Trade
Development Council. Photograph by Graham Uden.

"Trading floor of an international trading/investment company." Copyright © 2003
Hong Kong Trade Development Council. Photograph by Graham Uden.

"More than two million people in Hong Kong live in public housing estates, mostly
in Kowloon and the New Territories." Copyright © 2000 China Photo Library Ltd.

All reprinted by permission of Hong Kong Trade Development Council.

British Library Cataloguing-in-Publication Data
A catalogue record for this book is available from the British Library.

Secure On-line Ordering
http://www.hkupress.org

Printed and bound by Caritas Printing Training Centre, Hong Kong, China.

Hong Kong University Press is honoured that Xu Bing, whose art explores
the complex themes of language across cultures, has written the Press's
name in his Square Word Calligraphy. This signals our commitment to
cross-cultural thinking and the distinctive nature of our English-language
books published in China.

"At first glance, Square Word Calligraphy appears to be nothing more
unusual than Chinese characters, but in fact it is a new way of rendering
English words in the format of a square so they resemble Chinese
characters. Chinese viewers expect to be able to read Square Word
Calligraphy but cannot. Western viewers, however are surprised to find
they can read it. Delight erupts when meaning is unexpectedly revealed."
— Britta Erickson, *The Art of Xu Bing*

Contents

Preface

Hong Kong prides itself as a place where the economy is allowed to run with the minimum of government interference. Slogans ranging from the "positive non-intervention" of the 1970s to today's "maximum support and minimum intervention" and "market leads, government facilitates" epitomise the image which the government seeks to project. And the government is indeed highly sensitive about the way in which its style of economic management is perceived, both at home and abroad.

How accurate are those representations of the government's own role in the economy? Is Hong Kong truly the beacon of free-market, *laissez-faire* economics, as one might infer not only from the government's own propaganda, but also from the accolade of the world's freest economy which has repeatedly been bestowed upon Hong Kong by certain North American foundations? Even if the answer is yes, and *a fortiori* if it is no, how is economic policy formulated and who ultimately controls it?

These are the questions which this book explores and seeks to answer.

Part I provides some necessary background. Thus, Chapter 1 looks at Hong Kong's place in the world economy and its economic relationship with mainland China, which is by far Hong Kong's most important single counterpart in respect of trade and business. Chapter 2 then discusses the way in which Hong Kong projects itself to the outside world in terms of economic policies and, in turn, the way the outside world perceives it. That perception turns out to be, on balance, one of a free and reasonably competitive economic environment.

However, the justification for that view comes under challenge in Part II. By examining various aspects of economic management over the years, Chapter 3 reveals that the government in fact plays a rather significant role in directing economic activity. Chapter 4 focuses on budgetary policy, since this is the crucial channel for the financial decisions which give effect to much of economic policy. Hong Kong observes strict fiscal discipline, but the extent of fiscal intervention in the economy may be greater than the bare figures suggest. Chapter 5 looks in similar vein at monetary policy. In most economies of the world, monetary policy is used to fine-tune the economy, mainly just to maintain stable monetary conditions and low inflation, but in some instances in a more aggressive manner in pursuit of other goals. In Hong Kong monetary policy is almost entirely passive — a situation which tends to support the non-interventionist image. The focus of Chapter 6 is competition and competitiveness, as the necessary attributes of a prosperous economy. Although generally regarded as a competitive economy on the world stage, there is as yet no over-arching law in place to protect or promote competition, and several instances exist of weak competitive conditions, or worse, within the Hong Kong economy.

Overall, the government emerges as having rather more than just a minimal involvement in steering the economy. There has been a discernible tendency to seek to guide activity in specific directions. Part III turns to explore the formulation of economic policies in practice. Thus, Chapter 7 examines the relevant institutional framework and discusses the possible contributions of different organs of government, and other formal or quasi-formal channels, to policy-making in the economic sphere. Chapter 8 draws together the threads, and focuses on the informal but highly significant role of business leaders, in an attempt to identify how economic policies are developed and decided. A concluding section summarises the main findings of the book.

This book does not purport to present a comprehensive account of the entire Hong Kong economy. Rather, it selects a range of topics and examples which can help to illuminate the debate on the government's role in the economy, and which can contribute to assessing the significance of different players in the determination of economic policies. In so doing, it provides a quite wide, albeit partly selective, overview of economic policy and its formulation, which may be of interest to the general reader as much as to the student of Hong Kong's political economy.

The book goes to press as Hong Kong marks the tenth anniversary of its return to Chinese sovereignty, and as Donald Tsang, re-elected as chief executive, prepares his new team. There have been hints of new strategies and procedures, but only time will tell how the various issues raised in this book may evolve.

PART I

Status and Image

– 1 –

Economic Background

Prosperity and trade

Few people would challenge the assertion that Hong Kong has been a success story in terms of economic performance. In terms of gross domestic product per head, Hong Kong ranks either 27th or 8th in the world, depending on the method of currency conversion (see Table 1.1). One recognises, of course, that this is not a precise measure of standard of living, and does not necessarily reflect happiness or quality of life, but it remains one of the most widely accepted, uncomplicated bases for comparing economic performance.

In absolute terms, with a population of only some seven million, Hong Kong sits at only 35th or 40th place in rankings of economic size (again depending on the details of the calculation). This tends, however, to underestimate Hong Kong's importance to the international economy because of its disproportionately large role in trade. In that sense, Hong Kong is one of the world's most open economies, and, if statistics were available to compare not only openness in trade but also openness in finance, Hong Kong's significance on the world economic stage would undoubtedly be accentuated further.

An instructive comparison can be made with a country such as Switzerland, which ranks next to Hong Kong in terms of population, as well as in terms of the size of the economy judged by purchasing power, but which is, according to the calculations in Table 1.2, only about one quarter as 'open' in terms of external trade. This means that Switzerland is a relatively more self-contained economy, and is therefore less important to the rest of the world than is Hong Kong, and less dependent on it.

Table 1.1 Top 50 economies in terms of GDP and GDP per head, 2005*

	Gross domestic product			
Rank	calculated at market exchange rates; US$ billions		calculated at purchasing power parity rates; US$ billions	
1	United States	12,459	United States	12,278
2	Japan	4,567	China	9,412
3	Germany	2,792	Japan	3,910
4	China	2,234	India	3,633
5	United Kingdom	2,229	Germany	2,522
6	France	2,127	United Kingdom	1,833
7	Italy	1,766	France	1,830
8	Canada	1,132	Italy	1,668
9	Spain	1,127	Brazil	1,577
10	Brazil	796	Russia	1,576
11	South Korea	788	Canada	1,105
12	India	772	Spain	1,089
13	Mexico	768	Mexico	1,073
14	Russia	763	South Korea	994
15	Australia	709	Indonesia	977
16	Netherlands	630	Taiwan	631
17	Belgium	372	Australia	630
18	Switzerland	368	South Africa	570
19	Turkey	362	Turkey	569
20	Sweden	359	Iran	555
21	Taiwan	346	Thailand	545
22	Saudi Arabia	310	Argentina	534
23	Austria	305	Netherlands	503
24	Poland	303	Poland	496
25	Norway	296	Philippines	415
26	Indonesia	281	Pakistan	405
27	Denmark	260	Saudi Arabia	352
28	South Africa	239	Ukraine	338
29	Greece	226	Colombia	337
30	Ireland	200	Belgium	325
31	Finland	196	Bangladesh	306
32	Iran	192	Egypt	305
33	Portugal	184	Malaysia	291
34	Argentina	182	Austria	275
35	**Hong Kong**	**178**	Sweden	271
36	Thailand	173	Vietnam	252
37	Venezuela	133	Greece	249
38	Malaysia	131	Algeria	238
39	United Arab Emirates	130	Switzerland	237
40	Israel	130	**Hong Kong**	**233**
41	Czech Republic	124	Portugal	203
42	Colombia	122	Norway	195
43	Singapore	117	Chile	193
44	Chile	115	Romania	191
45	Pakistan	111	Denmark	188
46	Hungary	109	Czech Republic	188
47	New Zealand	109	Nigeria	174
48	Algeria	102	Hungary	170
49	Nigeria	99	Ireland	168
50	Romania	99	Peru	167

* Latest actuals or estimates, as at November 2006, from the International Monetary Fund's database for its 'World Economic Outlook', www.imf.org. Of the two exchange rate conversions, purchasing power parity may, in theory, provide the better basis for comparison, although its compilation in practice cannot be so precise

Table 1.1   Top 50 economies in terms of GDP and GDP per head, 2005* *(continued)*

Rank	Gross domestic product per head of population			
	calculated at market exchange rates; US$ per head		calculated at purchasing power parity rates; US$ per head	
1	Luxembourg	80,288	Luxembourg	69,800
2	Norway	64,193	Norway	42,364
3	Iceland	52,764	United States	41,399
4	Switzerland	50,532	Ireland	40,610
5	Ireland	48,604	Iceland	35,115
6	Denmark	47,984	Denmark	34,740
7	Qatar	43,110	Canada	34,273
8	United States	42,000	**Hong Kong**	**33,479**
9	Sweden	39,694	Austria	33,432
10	Netherlands	38,618	Switzerland	32,571
11	Finland	37,504	Qatar	31,397
12	Austria	37,117	Belgium	31,244
13	United Kingdom	37,023	Finland	31,208
14	Japan	35,757	Australia	30,897
15	Belgium	35,712	Netherlands	30,862
16	Canada	35,133	Japan	30,615
17	Australia	34,740	Germany	30,579
18	France	33,918	United Kingdom	30,436
19	Germany	33,854	Sweden	29,926
20	Italy	30,200	France	29,187
21	United Arab Emirates	27,700	Italy	28,534
22	Spain	27,226	Singapore	28,368
23	Singapore	26,836	United Arab Emirates	27,957
24	New Zealand	26,464	Taiwan	27,721
25	Kuwait	26,020	Spain	26,320
26	Brunei	25,754	Brunei	24,948
27	**Hong Kong**	**25,493**	New Zealand	24,797
28	Greece	20,327	Israel	23,474
29	Cyprus	20,214	Netherlands Antilles	22,750
30	Israel	19,248	Greece	22,392
31	Bahrain	18,403	Slovenia	21,808
32	Bahamas	18,062	Cyprus	21,177
33	Portugal	17,456	Bahrain	21,565
34	Netherlands Antilles	17,270	South Korea	20,590
35	Slovenia	16,986	Bahamas	20,076
36	South Korea	16,308	Malta	19,739
37	Taiwan	15,203	Portugal	19,335
38	Malta	13,803	Czech Republic	18,341
39	Saudi Arabia	13,410	Barbados	17,610
40	Oman	12,664	Oman	16,862
41	Trinidad & Tobago	12,625	Hungary	16,823
42	Czech Republic	12,152	Equatorial Guinea	16,507
43	Barbados	11,088	Estonia	16,414
44	Saint Kitts & Nevis	10,895	Kuwait	16,301
45	Hungary	10,814	Slovakia	16,041
46	Antigua & Barbuda	10,727	Saudi Arabia	15,229
47	Estonia	9,727	Saint Kitts & Nevis	14,649
48	Slovakia	8,775	Trinidad & Tobago	14,258
49	Croatia	8,675	Lithuania	14,158
50	Seychelles	8,556	Argentina	14,109

Table 1.2   Openness: Selected economies

Economy	Openness in trade
Australia	20
Austria	49
Belgium	83
Canada	36
China	34
Denmark	46
Finland	39
France	27
Germany	38
Hong Kong	192
Ireland	72
Italy	27
Japan	14
Luxembourg	149
Netherlands	66
New Zealand	29
Norway	37
Portugal	33
Singapore	227
Spain	28
Sweden	45
Switzerland	45
United Kingdom	28
United States	13

Source: *International Financial Statistics (IMF)*. Openness is measured by the average of imports and exports, of goods and services, as a percentage of gross domestic product. The figures mostly refer to 2005.

The China connection

The data in Table 1.2 underscore Hong Kong's role as an entrepot centre, and Hong Kong is essentially an entrepot for China, as illustrated in Table 1.3.

Table 1.3   Hong Kong's trade with China

Percentage of Hong Kong's total trade (imports plus exports and re-exports) which is with mainland China	
1938	42.7
1954	18.5
1979	10.6
2006	46.4

Source: *Hong Kong Statistics 1947–67, Hong Kong Annual Report 1980,* and web site of the Census and Statistics Department, Hong Kong government.

The figures in Table 1.3 serve as a reminder that Hong Kong's modern economy was largely founded on the China trade, which had reached some 43% of all Hong Kong's trade in goods just before the Second World War. The interruption of that war, followed by the communist revolution in China, followed a few years later by the Korean war and the associated embargos on certain forms of trade and financial dealings with China, caused Hong Kong's trade with China to slump. This downtrend continued through the upheavals of China's Great Leap Forward of 1958–62, and the Cultural Revolution which racked the country for some ten years from 1966. By 1979 China accounted for little more than 10% of Hong Kong's trade. That was the point at which Deng Xiaoping began to open up China's economy, and in 1980 the Shenzhen Special Economic Zone was established. Since then, the interdependence between Hong Kong and China has resurged, and by 2005 the share of mainland trade had at last surpassed the level at which it stood before the Second World War.

With the interruption, from the 1940s to the 1970s, of the previous dynamic economic relationship with the Mainland, and as a result of the flight of Chinese entrepreneurs to Hong Kong, Hong Kong developed its own flourishing manufacturing sector. During the 1960s and 1970s Hong Kong enjoyed a lead in the provision of cheap manufactured goods — clothing, toys and certain household products — to Western markets. Other southeast Asian countries joined Hong Kong in this, while Japan tended to focus more on cars and electrical goods. China was not yet a significant competitor. Over the last 20 years of the twentieth century, however, China emerged to dominate the very manufacturing in which Hong Kong had been specialising, and Hong Kong's own manufacturing businesses began to migrate across the border. In 1980, 23% of Hong Kong's GDP was being generated by manufacturing, and 68% by the service sectors. Today, little more than 3% comes from manufacturing, while services account for 90%. This contrast is particularly relevant when it comes to discussing the Hong Kong government's attempts to steer the development of the economy.

In the face of the erosion of its manufacturing activity, Hong Kong focused more on its earlier strength as a provider of entrepot services such as shipping and finance, and reasserted itself as the gateway to the Mainland. Geography, culture and history gave it something of a monopoly advantage. By today, however, that advantage has been considerably eroded by the direct accessibility of China itself to and from the wider world, and by China's own progress in developing such services.

Box 1.1 Hong Kong's economic interdependence with the Mainland

(Extracts from the official *Hong Kong Yearbook* for 2005, Chapter 3, reprinted by permission of the Government of the Hong Kong Special Administrative Region.)

The strengthening economic links between Hong Kong and the Mainland since the latter adopted the open door policy in 1978 have brought substantial mutual benefits. The flow of goods, services, people and capital between Hong Kong and the Mainland and between the Mainland and the world via Hong Kong have created a remarkable growth in income and employment opportunities in both Hong Kong and the Mainland over the years.

The Mainland has long been Hong Kong's largest trading partner, accounting for 45 per cent of the total trade value in Hong Kong in 2005. Ninety-one per cent of Hong Kong's re-export trade was related to the Mainland, making it the largest market for, as well as the largest source of, Hong Kong's re-exports. Reciprocally, Hong Kong was the Mainland's third largest trading partner (after the US and Japan), accounting for 10 per cent of the Mainland's total trade value in 2005.

Hong Kong is also a principal gateway to or from the Mainland for business and tourism. Between 1996 and 2005, the number of trips made by Hong Kong residents to the Mainland more than doubled, with an average annual growth rate of 9 per cent to 63 million trips. The number of trips made by foreign visitors to the Mainland through Hong Kong rose by a cumulative 77 per cent over the same period, with an average annual growth rate of 7 per cent to 4 million trips. In 2005, these two types of trips to the Mainland rose by 5 per cent and 10 per cent respectively. The number of trips made by Mainland residents to or through Hong Kong rose more than five fold, with an average annual growth rate of 20 per cent between 1996 and 2005 to 12.5 million trips. The growth moderated to 2 per cent in 2005, reflecting the slower growth in the Mainland's outbound tourism.

Hong Kong continues to be the largest external investor on the Mainland. According to the Mainland's statistics, the cumulative value of Hong Kong's realised direct investment on the Mainland reached US$260 billion at the end of 2005, accounting for 42 per cent of the total inward direct investment there. Over the years, there has been a noticeable shift in the composition of Hong Kong's direct investment across the boundary, from industrial processing to a wider spectrum of business ventures, such as hotels and tourist-related facilities, and real estate and infrastructure development. Compared to other places in the Mainland, Hong Kong's economic links with Guangdong are the closest. By the end of 2004, the cumulative value of Hong Kong's realised direct investment in Guangdong was US$100 billion, accounting for 66 per cent of its total inward direct investment.

According to a survey conducted by the Federation of Hong Kong Industries in December 2003, over 11 million Chinese workers were employed either directly or indirectly on the Mainland by industrial ventures with Hong Kong interests. This was about 62 times the size of Hong Kong's own manufacturing workforce. Within this total, about 10 million Chinese workers were employed in Guangdong. Hong Kong's huge direct investment in the Mainland has contributed to the latter's industrialisation, and at the same time facilitated the rapid structural change in the Hong Kong economy.

The Mainland is likewise Hong Kong's largest source of foreign direct investment (excluding tax haven economies).

Nevertheless, it is the role as a business platform for China that remains Hong Kong's most compelling attraction to overseas businesses and investors. Of course, many countries still have important trading interests with Hong Kong *per se* — Germany for cars, Australia and New Zealand for foodstuffs, Japan for cars and electronic goods. But the majority of foreigners nowadays see Hong Kong as an economic adjunct to mainland China, and will therefore stay committed, in business terms, to Hong Kong if, but only if, Hong Kong continues to present a business environment which is conducive to serving as a springboard to the Mainland.

Post-1997

The reversion to Chinese sovereignty in 1997 was a political milestone for Hong Kong rather than an economic one. Fears that it would lead to interference in economic policy and an erosion of the economic freedoms and free market principles for which Hong Kong had become famous have proved unfounded. The Basic Law — Hong Kong's mini-constitution — grants autonomy to Hong Kong in, among other things, economic, financial and monetary affairs. Among overseas observers who are not closely involved with Hong Kong, there may be a tendency to presume that China must surely play a significant role in directing economic policy, but polls of the people whose opinions are presumed to matter most, reveal that Hong Kong is still regarded as the world's freest economy (see Chapter 2). And the Mainland authorities appear to have been punctilious in formally respecting that autonomy granted by the Basic Law.

However, although the Mainland authorities have refrained from direct meddling in Hong Kong's economic policy, they have tended to regard economic prosperity as the key to political stability in Hong Kong — by which they mean, in effect, quiet compliance with their vision for the political evolution of Hong Kong. They do not want Hong Kong to pose any political problems for the Mainland as it pursues its own political evolution at its own chosen pace. Time and again, therefore, the Mainland authorities and the Hong Kong government have echoed one another with statements about the priority to be accorded to maintaining and increasing economic prosperity.

This, in turn, helps to explain the willingness of the Mainland authorities to exercise power and influence in order indirectly to help the Hong Kong economy, such as through the closer economic partnership arrangement (CEPA) and cooperative initiatives in the Pearl River region. Where such arrangements are likely to be mutually beneficial to both the Mainland and Hong Kong, there has been no reason for the Mainland authorities to hold back — for example, in admitting Hong Kong professionals to practise on the Mainland, as a way of upgrading the Mainland's own professional services at a controlled pace ahead of the fuller opening-up to the rest of the world which will eventually be required under China's obligations to the World Trade Organisation. But Hong Kong has found it less easy to wring concessions in areas where such steps could significantly threaten Mainland interests in terms of more intense competition, such as in the provision of local banking or telecommunication services.

At the same time, China has seen Hong Kong as a channel through which the Mainland economy can leverage its own performance. Mainland growth of the pace achieved over the past decade or so could probably not have been realised but for the role of Hong Kong in facilitating trade and development. But as China develops further its own services sector and its infrastructure, it will become less dependent on Hong Kong. This does not mean that Hong Kong will fade away, but rather that it must develop and assert its own intrinsic competitiveness.

Hong Kong itself has, of course, benefited hugely from the economic dynamism of its much larger neighbour, and been able to reap benefits from greater economic cooperation across the border. Many of the privileges which it has negotiated, such as under CEPA, would scarcely have been conceivable under British rule.

The five-year plan

The vision of the Mainland authorities remaining largely detached from economic decisions in Hong Kong needs, however, to be partially qualified by certain developments in 2006. Although Hong Kong is outside China's socialist system and therefore not subject to the planning which characterises Mainland economic policy, China's 11th 5-year plan included Hong Kong for the first time, referring to cooperation and exchanges in various fields; tacitly acknowledging the complementary role of Hong Kong in the Mainland's development, as well as the dependence of Hong Kong on China; and pledging Mainland support for maintaining Hong Kong as a centre for finance and trade. The mention of Hong Kong in the plan may be seen by some as a generous gesture of support, but by others as the possible beginnings of a more sinister intrusion. Developments so far in response to the plan tend, however, to allay any fears that it might mark the start of a significantly more hands-on approach to economic policy in Hong Kong, as is discussed further in Chapter 3.

The competitive challenge

While the prosperity of the Mainland has produced many positive spin-offs for Hong Kong, the Mainland's emergence now as an economy which can potentially compete in services as well as manufacturing has, as noted above, thrown a competitive challenge to Hong Kong. It is perhaps this, together with periods of recession in recent years, which has prompted the Hong Kong government to adopt what appears to have been a more proactive stance in managing the economy, with an emphasis on structural change. But similar structural challenges have confronted Hong Kong at different points in history — arguably almost continuously — and the government could be accused of having made too much of a meal of them in recent years. The ways in which government has been trying to direct the economy are analysed later, in Chapter 3.

– 2 –
Fretting over the Image:
External Perceptions and Relations

League tables

Hong Kong brands itself as 'Asia's world city' and is much concerned with its image and reputation to the outside world. Sometimes this concern seems to verge on paranoia.

Thus, the Hong Kong government takes great pride in having been in first place for more than ten years in the global league table of economic freedom produced by the Heritage Foundation, the US-based right-wing pressure group, and in having been ranked the world's freest economy for the past 35 years by the Cato Institute.

Table 2.1 summarises rankings taken from those and a variety of other sources, not all of which are quite so flattering.

Scores and league tables of this nature need to be viewed with a sizeable pinch of salt. Some, such as the Heritage Foundation's, are produced with a deliberate political agenda in mind. Others are rather narrowly focused in particular fields. All are open to debate as to the methodology. For example, the indicators used by the United Nations Conference on Trade and Development (UNCTAD) to assess inward investment performance are likely to favour small highly open economies, while its measurement of the friendliness of the environment for such investment includes somewhat contentious indicators such as energy consumption and mobile phone penetration. The World Bank's governance indicators are constructed with painstaking thoroughness, but the authors are themselves the first to admit to significant margins of error (which they even quantify in the source documentation). The Global Entrepreneurship Monitor gauges entrepreneurship essentially according to the formation of new firms, thereby

Table 2.1   A selection of rankings for Hong Kong

Compilers and reference years	Indicator	Hong Kong's ranking
Cato Institute & Fraser Institute,[a] 2004	world's freest economy	1st of 130
Heritage Foundation,[b] 2006	index of economic freedom	1st of 161
World Economic Forum,[c] 2006	overall global competitiveness	11th of 125
	growth competitiveness	28th of 117
	business competitiveness	10th of 121
International Institute for Management Development (Lausanne),[d] 2006	world competitiveness rankings	2nd of 60
Chinese Academy of Social Sciences,[e] 2005–06	urban competitiveness among cities in greater China	1st of 200
	global competitiveness among economies	11th of 100
UNCTAD,[f] averages,		
2003–05	performance of inward direct investment	3rd of 142
2002–04	potential for inward direct investment	15th of 142
2003–05	performance of outward direct investment	1st of 88
World Bank,[g] 2006	ease of doing business (prospectively in 2007)	5th of 175
World Bank,[h] 2005	governance-related indicators	*percentile rank (0–100) across 213 economies*
	'voice and accountability'	52.2
	'political stability'	89.6
	'government effectiveness'	92.8
	'regulatory quality'	100.0
	'rule of law'	91.3
	'control of corruption'	92.1
CLSA and Asia-Pacific & Asian Corporate Governance Association,[i] 2005	corporate governance in Asian economies	2nd of 10
Global Entrepreneurship Monitor,[j] 2004 *(London Business School and Babson College)*	total entrepreneurship activity	32nd of 34
Economist Intelligence Unit,[k] 2005	quality of business environment	8th of 82
	desirability as business trip location	39th of 127
Mercer Human Resource Consulting,[l] 2006	cost of living, cities	4th of 144
	quality of living, cities	68th of 350
UBS,[m] 2006	cost of living, cities	27th of 71
ECA International,[n] 2005–06	best city location in world for Asians	32nd of 257
	best in world for west Europeans	66th
	best in Asia for Asians	5th

Sources: [a] 'Economic Freedom of the World', www.cato.org; www.fraserinstitute.ca.
  [b] Index of economic freedom, www.heritage.org.
  [c] 'Global Competitiveness Report 2006–2007', www.weforum.org.
  [d] 'IMD World Competitiveness Yearbook 2006', www.imd.ch.
  [e] As reported by Xinhua news agency, 23 March 2006, www.china.org.cn.
  [f] UNCTAD 'World Investment Report 2006', www.unctad.org.
  [g] 'Doing business 2007. How to reform', World Bank Group, www.doingbusiness.org.
  [h] 'Worldwide Governance Indicators: 1996–2005', www.worldbank.org.
  [i] www.acga-asia.org.
  [j] www.gemconsortium.org.
  [k] 'Viewswire' for Hong Kong, www.viewswire.com; and 'The world in 2006', www.economist.com.
  [l] 'Cost of living survey' and 'Quality of living survey', Mercer Human Resource Consulting, www.mercerhr.com.
  [m] 'Prices and earnings: A comparison of purchasing power around the globe', 2006 edition, www.ubs.com; comparison based on western European consumption patterns.
  [n] Press release of 3 April 2006, www.eca-international.com.

biasing towards less mature economies or those experiencing profound structural change, while ignoring innovative activity from within existing companies. The Chinese Academy warns that other Chinese cities are catching up rapidly on Hong Kong's lead. Employment Conditions Abroad (ECA) explains that although Hong Kong scores well on law and order and good governance, it loses out because of poor air quality and the scares in recent years over incidents such as SARS and avian flu. Space does not allow a full analysis of methodologies; those readers who are interested may wish to refer to the relevant sources.

What emerges from these surveys as a whole is a picture of a place which scores very well on economic freedom and pretty well in terms of the business environment and competitiveness, but rather less well on perceived quality of life.

Hong Kong officials make much play of these results, when favourable. For example, when the results from the Fraser Institute and the Cato Institute were announced in September 2005, Hong Kong's financial secretary immediately issued a press release welcoming Hong Kong's rating as the world's freest economy.[1]

However, when the findings are less favourable, there is a tendency to query the methodology, or to work behind the scenes to 'educate' the compilers. Thus when, also in September 2005, the World Economic Forum relegated Hong Kong from 7th to 28th in its rankings of 'growth competitiveness', the acting financial secretary told a reporter:

> I think a lot of these institutions may not have a very good, clear understanding of Hong Kong. They may have miscalculated the points. We will be talking with these people in the near future to bring about a better understanding of where we are.[2]

Such efforts may, however, be misdirected since, although 'growth competitiveness' may sound like a fairly objective concept, the index is in fact based significantly on the subjective perceptions of business people. The World Economic Forum's researchers have simply observed and collated those views, and cannot be held to account for the shifting perceptions of their interviewees. Interestingly, Hong Kong stood second in this ranking in 1997. The decline since then may have owed something to concerns arising from Beijing's moves to reverse or pre-empt Hong Kong court rulings on right of abode, and some rather heavy-handed finger-wagging from Beijing, albeit mostly from only middle or lower-ranking officials, about such issues as the pace of democratic reform. Such developments may be imperfectly understood in the international business community. It is a major challenge for the Hong Kong government to dispel any patently mistaken perceptions that may exist.

Credit-rating agencies

There is a similar craving to be held in high esteem by the leading credit-rating agencies such as Moody's, Standard and Poor's, and Fitch. Hong Kong officials have worked unashamedly and, one might conclude, with some evident success, to persuade those agencies to adopt what the government would describe as a more balanced view of Hong Kong, and, in particular, to acknowledge Hong Kong as separate from China for rating purposes. The following is an extract from the Hong Kong Monetary Authority's annual report:

> The HKMA has been playing a pivotal role in the adoption of a more proactive approach towards international credit rating agencies on Hong Kong's credit ratings. Through more effective communication between the international credit rating agencies and the relevant authorities, the HKMA aims at ensuring that the agencies maintain a more balanced view on Hong Kong. Amid improved economic prospects in Hong Kong, these efforts have paid off. Between April and June, Standard & Poor's, Fitch Ratings, and Rating and Investment Information all upgraded the outlook on Hong Kong's sovereign rating from negative to stable.[3]

In similar vein is the following account from the financial secretary's visit to the United States in September 2005:

> During the visit, Mr Tang had meetings with two major credit rating agencies, namely Moody's Investor Services and Standard and Poor's, to update them on Hong Kong's continued broad-based economic recovery and impressive improvements in our fiscal positions to ensure that they will take all relevant factors into consideration and arrive at fair and accurate ratings for Hong Kong.[4]

In view of such efforts, it is hardly surprising that the government should be seen preening itself whenever the agencies comment favourably. Thus, for example, the decisions by Standard and Poor's in April 2006 and again in July 2006 to upgrade Hong Kong's foreign currency and local currency ratings were both greeted instantly by self-congratulatory government press releases, headlined "Government welcomes S&P's decision to upgrade HK's ratings".[5]

It remains something of a mystery why the government feels it necessary to issue a formal comment virtually every time that some external agency or research body makes a reference to Hong Kong. There can be few other governments that admit so openly to their efforts to obtain high approval ratings, and which display such childlike pleasure when the results are favourable, or pique when unfavourable.

International organisations

The government is also sensitive to comment or criticism from official international bodies. For example, it has, over the years, staunchly defended its position on competition policy against thinly disguised criticism from the World Trade Organisation (WTO) and International Monetary Fund (IMF).

Thus, the WTO, in its Trade Policy Review for Hong Kong of December 2002, was critical of the fact that the government, in its 1998 statement on competition policy, did not define exactly what it meant by anti-competitive practices, and that the statement did not mention any provisions regarding mergers and acquisitions. Without these, the WTO remarked, it was "unclear how the Government can (transparently) prevent changes in HKSAR's industrial structure that could be detrimental to consumer welfare and to competition itself." The Review went on to comment that it was not clear how Hong Kong officials could be expected to identify anti-competitive practices if there were no statutes defining them.

The IMF subsequently referred to the debate in the following terms:

> The WTO [recently] expressed concern that high firm concentration in certain sectors, and the absence of a comprehensive competition law, may hinder business investment by local and foreign firms. . . . The [Hong Kong] authorities noted that, while remaining committed to the sector-specific approach to competition policy, they were also keeping a watch on possible anti-competitive behaviours, with a view to ensuring fair competition in the non-regulated sectors and introducing additional sector-specific measures to promote competition if necessary.[6]

The slight tension over any potentially prescriptive IMF interference is apparent if one reads between those lines. Significantly, however, the Hong

Kong government has recently shown signs of succumbing to international pressure on the competition front.[7] Meanwhile, whenever the IMF delivers any favourable or supportive comments, the Hong Kong government is quick to make play of them. A typical illustration is the government's press release in February 2006, after the IMF's annual scrutiny of the Hong Kong economy, headlined: "IMF commends Hong Kong's macroeconomic management".[8]

Britain

The British government maintains a continuing interest in Hong Kong, to ensure that the terms of the Sino-British Joint Declaration of 1984 are being adhered to. This merits a mention here because the British secretary of state for foreign and commonwealth affairs presents a report on Hong Kong to the UK Parliament every six months. The importance of the British government's commentaries is not simply that they express the views of the former colonial power, but that they carry weight in diplomatic circles around the world, particularly in countries which do not maintain a capability to monitor Hong Kong closely for themselves. On one occasion the report expressed concern over the intervention of the Mainland authorities regarding the pace and scope of constitutional development, which seemed inconsistent with the high degree of autonomy guaranteed to Hong Kong by the Joint Declaration.[9] But, in the context of this book, there has never been any contentious comment on the conduct of economic policy.

The issue at stake

This chapter has revealed Hong Kong as a rather self-conscious place. It cherishes its image as a free-market economy, with minimal government interference beyond the requirements of a sound legal and regulatory framework. It does not take too kindly to criticism.

The image of Hong Kong as the archetypal exponent of minimal government intervention is, however, oversimplistic. Any government is necessarily involved in its economy to a certain extent, if only to provide infrastructure and public services. In Hong Kong, the government's involvement actually goes rather further than that, as will be explored in Part II.

PART II

Economic Policies and Their Application

- 3 -

Government Involvement in the Economy: Words and Actions

Overview

The government has a somewhat ambivalent view of its own role in the economy. It adopts various slogans, such as 'positive non-interventionism' (first coined by Philip Haddon-Cave, who was financial secretary from 1971 to 1981), 'maximum support and minimum intervention' and 'market leads, government facilitates' (the catchphrase of the recent financial secretary, Henry Tang). It holds that it does not seek to direct or plan the course that the economy should take, since investors and entrepreneurs are deemed to understand markets far better than officials. Haddon-Cave, one of the most forthright champions of the *laissez-faire* philosophy, considered that government should not be involved at all in promoting, protecting or subsidising any particular economic activities,[10] but his successor, John Bremridge, once declared that he was "not philosophically opposed to government intervention in industry".[11]

The overall impression of its credo, imparted by successive administrations over the years, has been that government's fundamental role in the economic policy context is merely to provide the most business-friendly conditions possible, and a level playing field. In practice, however, the degree of detachment is not as great as the declared stance and the headline slogans might suggest.

The official view

To understand, in a bit more detail, the government's overall vision for the economy as it stands today, one may start by considering the government's own declaration of its economic strategy (Box 3.1).

Box 3.1 The official line on the economy and economic policy

(Extracts from the official *Hong Kong Yearbook* for 2004, Chapter 3, reprinted by permission of the Government of the Hong Kong Special Administrative Region.)

The Government of the HKSAR believes in free markets, and adopts "market leads, government facilitates" as the guiding principle of its economic policy. Over the past few years, the Government has taken a proactive role to create a conducive environment for business and facilitate economic development, so to enhance Hong Kong's competitiveness and reduce rigidities in the economy. While these measures aim at a longer-term target, they also aided the swift revival of the Hong Kong economy after SARS [severe acute respiratory syndrome which struck Hong Kong in 2003].

Proximity to the Mainland as a huge and dynamic economic hinterland is a key edge that Hong Kong possesses over neighbouring economies. Over the past two decades, economic relations between the two places continued to strengthen. Bilateral trade has grown by leaps and bounds. Two-way visitor flows have surged, more so upon the Mainland's progressive liberalisation on residents travelling abroad. Hong Kong and the Mainland are each other's largest source of external direct investment. In the financial sector, cross-boundary fund flows have risen markedly over the years. Hong Kong is an important fund raising centre for Mainland's state-owned enterprises and recently private enterprises.

Hong Kong aims to reap the enormous opportunities being accorded by rapid growth and further liberalisation in the Mainland economy, while making effective use of its international business perspective to meet the Mainland's development needs. Thus, it is essential to foster the inter-flows of people, goods, capital, information and services between the two places.

The signing of CEPA was a major milestone in improving the economic interface between Hong Kong and the Mainland. CEPA adopts a building block approach whereby more measures will be added as necessary. On trade in goods, the zero tariff concession on Hong Kong's domestic exports effective since January 1, 2004, has helped lift the competitiveness of Hong Kong's products in the Mainland market, as compared with products imported from other places. On trade in services, by giving Hong Kong companies a 'first mover' advantage in a large number of sectors, CEPA should facilitate expansion of Hong Kong's services across the boundary and open up more opportunities for business in the Mainland. Trade and investment facilitation will help promote and streamline trade, investment and other business flows between the two places.

The launch and progressive extension of the Individual Visit Scheme for Mainland residents coming to Hong Kong has added fuel to the already strong upturn in Mainland visitor inflow. In 2004, there were nearly 4.3 million Mainland visitors to Hong Kong under this scheme, accounting for only one-third of the growth in overall visitor arrivals from this source. This is rendering an important invigorating force to Hong Kong's inbound tourism.

Focusing on areas where Hong Kong has clear comparative advantages is the only way to compete with the rest of the world. Financial services; trading and logistics; tourism; and producer and professional services are the sectors that give Hong Kong this edge. They are not only the key drivers of Hong Kong's economic growth, they have also been providing the main impetus to job creation. In 2003, these key industries taken together contributed to 54.9 per cent of GDP and 44.3 per cent in terms of total employment.

Over the past year [2004], a number of measures have been put in place to foster the development of these key industries. To develop Hong Kong as an international financial centre, measures were initiated to improve our regulatory regime and reinforce corporate governance of listed companies and professional standards of intermediaries. The securitisation of government toll tunnels and bridges has helped promote development of the bond market and generated one-off revenue for government coffers. To enhance Hong Kong's position as a regional logistics centre, airline services were progressively liberalised, and measures were implemented to reduce cross-boundary trucking costs in order to enhance the efficiency of our port services. The HKSAR Government has drawn up a concept plan on development of Lantau for public consultation with a view to strengthening Hong Kong's position as a regional transportation, logistics and tourism hub.

The Hong Kong economy has also benefited from several policy measures initiated by the Central Government in 2004. In early 2004, the Central Government agreed to enable Hong Kong's local banks to operate personal renminbi business, including deposit, exchange, remittances and renminbi bank cards. This enhanced the role of Hong Kong as a key financial centre for the Mainland. In August, measures were introduced to facilitate Mainland enterprises investing in Hong Kong and Macao. The Central Government's other relaxation measures, though not exclusive to Hong Kong, will also benefit the Hong Kong economy by facilitating the inflow of Mainland capital. For instance, Mainland insurance companies are now allowed to invest in overseas capital markets, and it is reckoned that Hong Kong will be the key beneficiary. Hong Kong also stands to benefit from relaxation of restrictions on outward remittance associated with emigration of Mainland residents and Mainland students studying overseas, and from the raising of the limit on renminbi cash Mainlanders are allowed to carry on overseas trips.

The vision of the HKSAR Government is to develop Hong Kong as Asia's world city by consolidating Hong Kong's unique position in the region as well as its role as a gateway to the Mainland. Reflecting the prominent role of Hong Kong as a business hub in the region, the number of overseas and Mainland companies to set up operations in Hong Kong has continued to rise in recent years, more so after the launch of CEPA. Specifically, the number of regional headquarters and regional offices in Hong Kong in 2004 hit new highs. Within this total, the number of regional headquarters set up by Mainland companies in Hong Kong had a more distinct increase, as many of these Mainland companies set up business operations or joined forces with local enterprises to tap the vast market potential of CEPA. The envisaged benefits of setting up operations in Hong Kong under CEPA are also one of the factors considered by many overseas companies in investing in Hong Kong.

The quotation comes from the government's own comprehensive overview of Hong Kong, written in 2005, and is reproduced here in full in order to convey a sense of the overall balance in the government's thinking on the economy.

What emerges is a very marked emphasis on the leverage which Hong Kong has achieved, and hopes further to exploit, from the Mainland economy. This benefit is in part the happily unavoidable result of Hong Kong's economy being already quite well attuned to its large and rapidly growing neighbour. But it also reflects intensive efforts by the Hong Kong administration to gain better access to the Mainland market in both goods and services. This is manifest in CEPA (of which more below) as well as, for example, in the acquiescence of the Mainland authorities to certain amounts of renminbi banking business being conducted in Hong Kong. It would be wrong to regard all of this as signifying an attempt to manage or plan the economy. Rather it represents the successful negotiation of the removal of barriers to trade and to business, for the specific benefit of Hong Kong, generally some years in advance of the liberalisation that will proceed on a broader front as a result of China's membership of the World Trade Organisation.

The quoted passage also evidences the government's commitment to a market-based economy, with an active approach towards maintaining a business-friendly and business-facilitative environment, together with appropriate infrastructure.

But there can only ever be a rather fine dividing line between, on the one hand, facilitating in a neutral sense and, on the other, coaxing or subsidising in a statist manner. For example, building roads is generally accepted as necessary infrastructure, for which government should take responsibility. But if a certain stretch of road is seen overwhelmingly to serve a particular company or sector, the government may be judged to be adopting a selective industrial policy.

The call for a focus on four areas where Hong Kong has a clear comparative advantage comes close to interventionism. Not only does it presume of the administration a skill in identifying comparative advantage in, necessarily, a forward-looking sense, but it is also suggestive of something more than mere exhortation. There is an implication that the administration will, or would like to, direct resources to those sectors. Such efforts at 'picking winners' can be frought with danger, as will be discussed later. And that sort of statement somewhat tarnishes the avowal that Hong Kong is fully committed to free-market principles.

In fact, there have been some very specific episodes of government intervention in the economy over the years — with mixed results, as will be elaborated in the following sections.

Industrial estates and similar initiatives

One of the clearest, early signs of a departure from pure *laissez-faire* and a move towards a more dirigiste mentality came in the 1970s when the concept of industrial estates evolved. This was at the time when high land prices were beginning to impact upon Hong Kong's competitiveness in certain sectors. And soon the first concrete signs of China's competitive strength as a manufacturing base were to emerge, in particular with the establishment of the Shenzhen Special Economic Zone in 1980. Factory owners in Hong Kong began to look across the border for much lower-cost locations, based on cheap sites and on wage costs a fraction of those in Hong Kong.

To this day, even though Hong Kong has demonstrated, and benefited from, a distinct comparative advantage in services — notably as a complement to the Mainland's industrial development — the government has continued to hanker after preserving and nurturing some manufacturing within Hong Kong.

Thus the administration took a conscious decision to try to retain manufacturing in Hong Kong, but dressed this up as a push for high technology activity. Moreover, the government plainly believed that it was doing no more than 'facilitating' — though there is scope for a semantic debate about the distinction between facilitating and subsidising. The principle became established of providing land to qualifying firms on the basis of their paying for the land at cost-price (much of it was formed by reclamation from the sea or marshland) rather than the market price.

There are now three industrial estates. The first two were at Tai Po and Yuen Long. A third, at Tseung Kwan O, was added later. They cover, together, a total of almost 200 hectares. The original criterion for land grants on the estates was that the applicant business should be of a manufacturing nature, which would be at the forefront of technology but which could not function satisfactorily in the multi-storey factory blocks where most of Hong Kong's traditional manufacturing was located.

From the start, there was difficulty in validating the tenancies on the estates against the high-tech criterion which had been set. In practice, a significant number of tenants have been in such superficially low-tech activities as food processing, brewing, printing, building materials, and so on. But there is always scope to introduce the very latest technologies to any activity, and that is essentially what provided many of the justifications. This was seen also as a justification for admitting some businesses which were essentially service operations.

The estate tenants enjoyed the benefit of staying close to their Hong Kong customers and to their Hong Kong shipment facilities, together with a subsidised land cost. In more recent years, land grants on the estates have been approved for such ventures as satellite monitoring stations and optical fibre manufacture, as well as the manufacture of traditional Chinese medicines. The estates management has endeavoured to follow a cluster approach, with, for example, food and communications in Tai Po, logistics and building services in Yuen Long, and more service-orientated activities in Tseung Kwan O.

That was the beginning. Then, in 1991 the British colonial governor announced the establishment of the Industry and Technology Development Council. The mid-1990s saw further land set aside for high-tech or new-tech industry, and incentives given to upgrade technology. The Applied Research Centre was established and the seeds were sown for what is now the Science and Technology Park.

The official support for such moves, while the government remained ostensibly committed to the free market, was rationalised by the financial secretary in his 1994 budget speech:

> There is little point in using taxpayers' money in pursuit of policies which go against the economic tide. Nevertheless, there will continue to be scope for helping our manufacturing industry move up-market — hence the injection of funds into the Innovation and Technology Development Council, into the new industrial estate at Tseung Kwan O and into the new Industry Technology Centre Corporation, all to help us move up the technological ladder.

The logic was not entirely convincing; no evidence was produced to show that the flow of "the economic tide" was in fact in this direction.

Paradoxically, at about the same time there was a growing realisation that services would be the main impetus for the economy in future. The Hong Kong Tourist Association (HKTA) was receiving government support, as was the Convention and Exhibition Centre. In 1996 the government made a grant to HKTA to set up a Tourism Development Fund. A Task Force on Services Promotion — a purely advisory and promotional body, but symptomatic of the importance now afforded to services — was set up, and produced a Framework for Action. Yet the financial secretary declared: "We need to be very cautious about committing public funds to support what are essentially commercial projects." Even so, he established a services support fund and handed some extra cash to the HKTA.

Further dirigiste tendencies

By now there was emerging a danger of the government being all too pervasive in its involvement with the economy. Public housing, roads, railways and the airport, schools and hospitals were all uncontentious fields of government involvement. But the initiatives here and there to assist specific industries and services were, arguably, increasingly inconsistent with the basic philosophy which Hong Kong espoused.

The dirigiste atmosphere intensified when Tung Chee Hwa became chief executive after the 1997 handover. But he may not have been entirely to blame. At the very least, he could find a shred of justification in the Basic Law — Hong Kong's new mini-constitution under Chinese sovereignty. In fact the Basic Law gives a mixed message. Despite its general support for the free market economy, it appears to leave the way open for some intervention. Article 118 says that the government should provide an "environment for encouraging investments, technological progress and the development of new industries", while Article 119 places on government a duty to "formulate appropriate policies to promote and coordinate the development of various trades such as manufacturing, commerce, tourism, real estate, transport, public utilities, services, agriculture and fisheries".

Whereas Article 118 appears to lay some emphasis on supply-side policies, Article 119 could be read as a charter for meddling in all sorts of economic activities. The intention of the drafters of the Basic Law might indeed have been to encourage the post-colonial administration to be involved more extensively in economic management than its British predecessors. On the other hand, with such an exhaustive list as given in Article 119, it could simply be interpreted as a generalised instruction to pursue sensible economic policies.[12]

Whatever the intention, Tung Chee Hwa behaved as if he had the green light to be more interventionist. The tone of his annual policy addresses in the years that followed was very much one of identifying activities which were deemed important — in many cases important enough to warrant some injection of public funding. Thus, in his first address he followed the unexceptional generalisation that "the way forward is to develop high value-added industries and services", with the identification of particular target sectors. These were: travel and tourism, with a $100 million loan to the HKTA; film, music and broadcasting, with the grant of a land site for film production; manufacturing; and high-tech business in general, for which the Applied Research Fund would receive additional funding. The aim, he declared, was to make Hong Kong a centre for innovation. Firm plans for a science park were announced, as was the setting up of the Commission on Strategic Development — sounding very much like a planning body, albeit only billed as an advisory one.

The presumption that it is somehow the government's duty to steer the direction of economic development was again evident in the 1998 policy address:

> Hong Kong must now chart a new course and find a new niche . . . consider how to reinforce our role as a bridge between China and the international community, as well as how to enhance our function as a leading business centre . . .

All of that was general enough, but the chief executive went on to identify innovation and technology as engines of growth, and thence to direct official support and funding for an Industrial Technology Centre, more cash for the Applied Research Fund, an Industry Support Fund, a Science Park, and establishment of the Hong Kong Productivity Council.

There followed in that address a long list of goals and desiderata, including: to become a world fashion and design centre; a regional centre for multi-media-based information and entertainment services; a world centre for the development of food and pharmaceuticals based on Chinese medicine; and a regional centre for professional and technological talents and services. And, recognising research and development as an area of weakness, initiatives were launched to create an Applied Science and Technological Research Institute (subsequently established in 2001) and an Innovation and Technology Fund. He also stated that "Continued development of the manufacturing sector must be a matter of priority". Subsequently, in the

1998 budget, the financial secretary announced, in that context, an extra $1 billion for research and productivity improvement schemes.

Jumping forward a few years, it is worth noting that the government's Applied Research Fund — in effect government-sponsored venture capital — proved something of a disaster, frittering away large sums in operating expenses ($103 million up to 2005) and having to write off over half of the sums which it invested. The government subsequently announced that it would be wound up by 2008. Significantly, the innovation and technology commissioner, Anthony Wong Sik-kei, referred to the incompatibility of its "public mission to develop Hong Kong's high-tech industry" with "the requirement that it bring financial returns".[13]

The Innovation and Technology Fund has proved equally controversial, reporting to the Legislative Council in 2005 that only 157 of 349 completed projects were useful or benefited the related industries. There is more than a hint here of pursuing technology for its own sake, rather than for the economic returns that it ought to reap.

The Science and Technology Park is located near to the Chinese University, on a waterside site between Shatin and Tai Po, and was officially opened in June 2002. A number of companies have been successfully attracted to locate their research and development activities there. New firms are given encouragement under a business incubation scheme, from which they can in due course graduate to be full tenants. A Bio-Informatics Centre, based at the park, was created in 2004 to serve as a nexus for research and development in biotechnology, Chinese medicine and other related health fields.

Finally, the so-called InnoCentre was set up in Kowloon Tong. This aims to provide a one-stop shop for design activities.

In 2001 the industrial estates, science park and InnoCentre were brought together under a single umbrella body, the Hong Kong Science and Technology Parks Corporation. By March 2006, of the industrial estates, 59% of the space available at Tseung Kwan O and 98% at the other two was occupied, as was 89% of space in Phase I of the Science Park and 98% at the InnoCentre.

The Corporation regards the parks as infrastructural development, in the same vein as hospitals or schools, not as a commercial project. This is seen to justify dependency on public funding. Although the intention is to wean the Corporation away from subsidies, the sunk costs are unlikely to be recovered and the overall return on the government's outlays is unlikely to reach a commercial level. It may in the near future show an operating surplus in its accounts, but this will only arise if government grants are written off. In terms of opportunity cost, taking account of the gift of the land on what would otherwise be valuable residential or commercial sites, the subsidies towards construction, and the fact that the corporation sets rents more with a view to being competitive with other regional analogues, than with regard to market rentals in Hong Kong, the entire exercise seems hard to justify in strict cost-benefit terms.

Cyberport and Disneyland

Tung Chee Hwa's policy address in 1999 again took up his theme of new challenges. Indeed this type of rhetoric was to characterise all the policy addresses of his tenure. The 1999 address was noteworthy for the launch of two initiatives which were to prove particularly controversial: Disneyland and Cyberport. Both involved a substantial commitment of public funds (or revenue forgone).

The Cyberport project centred on the negotiated grant of land to a single development company which would develop a cybernetics business centre providing 95,000 m² of 'intelligent' office space, but would also be able to undertake very substantial residential development for its own account. The granting of the project was not open to competition. This turned out to be a key point of controversy, especially in view of the fact that the chosen developer was Pacific Century Cyberworks, part of the business empire of Li Ka Shing and his family, reputedly the wealthiest and most influential business leader in Hong Kong.

The project was conceived at the height of the dot-com boom, when many of Hong Kong's regional neighbours had already built, or were in the process of building, their own facilities to foster and support the development of information technology. Hong Kong feared being left behind. Government was concerned as to how to prevent that. The prior question of whether, in the realms of comparative advantage and structural evolution of the economy, Hong Kong really needed a strong 'cyber' sector does not appear to have been properly addressed.

The project was subsequently justified by the financial secretary in his budget speech thus:

Having identified information services as a target, we must look for development in this area which will upgrade our existing economic activities, create new products, and expose them to the electronic world market.

He added that Cyberport would create a cluster of firms to

specialise in the development of services and multi-media content to support businesses and industries ranging from financial services, through trading, advertising and entertainment, to communications.

Further insights can be gleaned from Cyberport's own publicity, some of which has a somewhat hollow resonance today (Box 3.2).

Box 3.2   Cyberport's declared aims

(Quotation taken from the Cyberport website, www.cyberport.com.hk)

Establish Hong Kong Cyberport as a leading information technology hub and digital city of the Asia-Pacific region.

- To create a strategic cluster of quality IT and IT related companies critical to the development of Hong Kong into a leading digital city in the region;
- To nurture and support the development of small and medium IT enterprises as an essential constituent of such a strategic cluster;
- To provide a state-of-the-art infrastructure conducive to the creation of such a strategic cluster and its development;
- To develop a regional center of excellence for IT and digital media training for creating human capital in IT through collaboration and partnership with the industry, academia, and research institutes and professional bodies;
- To spearhead the development of the digital media industry through the provision of hardware, software and technical support in the Digital Media Centre; and
- To promote the development of services and applications for wireless and mobile communications leveraging on Cyberport's excellent infrastructure and synergy.

Meanwhile, the government's own account of how the project evolved provides a telling story of the way in which consultants can be brought in to validate an official plan (Box 3.3).

Box 3.3 The official justification for Cyberport

(Extracts from an article by the secretary for commerce, industry and technology, John Tsang Chun-wah, *South China Morning Post*, 26 January 2005, reprinted by permission of Mr John Tsang Chun-wah.)

. . . the Pacific Century Group (PCG), now called PCCW, presented to government the Cyberport concept, suggesting the government should construct Cyberport as a public works project with PCG as one of the anchor tenants. Naturally, without any upfront commitment from leading IT companies that they would move into Cyberport, the government was unwilling to commit from public coffers the substantial capital cost necessary to develop the project. Also, it has always been the government's intention to have the private sector take a lead in the development of projects of this nature.

Later in 1998, PCG put forward a revised proposal that included an ancillary residential development to provide revenue to finance the project. PCG would also be responsible for constructing the Cyberport portion, which comprised offices and supporting facilities, and would hand them over to government upon completion. In other words, the government would be the sole owner of the Cyberport portion, in addition to sharing the surplus sales proceeds from the residential portion.

To ascertain the benefits of Cyberport to Hong Kong, the government engaged an international consultant Arthur Andersen Business Consulting — to conduct a strategic assessment of the proposal. The consultant concluded that a development such as Cyberport would be an important element of Hong Kong's economic infrastructure, that it could assist IT companies by providing state-of-the-art facilities at shared cost, and that it could give Hong Kong an international marketing advantage in enhancing its image and competitiveness as an international information services centre. The government's decision to proceed with the

Cyberport project was thus in line with the global trend of creating IT clusters and nurturing professional talent in strategic information infrastructure.

Further studies by the consultant confirmed that there was across-the-board support from the local IT sector for the Cyberport concept. By the end of 2001, more than 70 applications for office tenancy had been received, but the subsequent bursting of the dot.com bubble shattered many dreams. By the time the Cyberport portion was completed in mid-2004, more than one-third of the first batch of applicant companies had disappeared and others had dramatically altered their business plans.

The consultants' conclusions can effectively be paraphrased thus: "If you, as a government, want to put money into this sort of activity, your Cyberport plan is as good a way as any of doing so." There was no discussion of the opportunity cost, nor identification of any wider economic benefits. Cyberport might be an important element in the economic infrastructure, but would it be an efficient usage of resources? And the dangers of simply following a global trend were amply demonstrated by subsequent events. Finally, it was obviously disingenuous to employ the fact that there was support from the IT sector as an argument for proceeding with an IT project.

Cyberport also caused some friction with the Science and Technology Parks Corporation because of some perceived overlap in objectives, at a time when the science park itself was struggling to attract interest. Reportedly, in the scramble for a similar range of IT tenants, marketing teams from Science Park and Cyberport were battling head-to-head with promotional incentives such as limited rent-free periods to prospective tenants.

In the event, the residential property portion of the Cyberport development has flourished while the business side has struggled to reach any sort of critical mass in cyber activities. The management company stated in October 2006 that the commercial premises were 73% occupied, but it is unclear how much of this represents actual 'cyber' activity. Meanwhile, the government's earlier slogan of Hong Kong as "the cyber city for the cyber century"[14] has been quietly set aside.

The Hong Kong Disneyland project was announced in November 1999 as a joint venture between The Walt Disney Company and the Hong Kong SAR government. The theme park opened in September 2005. Here again there was a large public subsidy in the grant of land and installation of infrastructure, and the financial arrangements meant that the government carried disproportionately the risks of the project. Critics have wondered why, if the sponsors were so certain of success, private enterprise could not have taken on the entire project. Only time will tell. Perhaps the government will reap a bonanza, but attendance figures for the first year or so appeared to fall short of target.

One factor which seemed to have been largely overlooked in the Disney calculation was the burden on associated infrastructure, such as road, rail and border crossings, as well as on society, which might arise, given the large numbers of comparatively low budget visitors, overwhelmingly from the Mainland, who were predicted, correctly, to be the main patrons. Another consideration which appeared to be overlooked was the possible extent to which Disneyland might be seen to take Hong Kong down-market as a visitor destination, engulfing tourist facilities with low-spending visitors while potentially scaring away some of the higher-spending tourists.

An interesting aspect from the economic policy perspective is the way in which, almost simultaneously, the high-tech Cyberport project and the comparatively low-tech tourist attraction of Disneyland were said to be identified as areas where Hong Kong had a comparative advantage which needed official help to manifest itself.

In October 1999, in a document titled "Ground Rules for Special Consideration of Private Sector Initiatives",[15] the government stated that,

> As a general rule, bureaus and departments will continue to consider and process proposed projects initiated by the private sector in accordance with approved government policies and procedures. They will continue to follow an open, fair and competitive bidding process for the disposal of land and the procurement of goods and services. Any departure from the norm must be fully justified on a case-by-case basis, having regard to the merits of the specific proposal.

Neither Cyberport nor Disneyland followed fully competitive and transparent procedures, and neither project was open to advance public discussion. Cyberport has been the more vilified as a result; Disneyland somewhat less so, perhaps because it enjoys more popular appeal.

Struggling with conscience

The then financial secretary, Donald Tsang, was plainly wrestling with his conscience about the extent of government intervention when, in his 2000 budget speech, he quoted the following words of one of his predecessors, Philip Haddon-Cave, some 20 years earlier:

> It is normally futile and damaging to the growth rate of an economy, particularly an open economy, for the Government to attempt to plan the allocation of resources available to the private sector and to frustrate the operation of market forces, no matter how uncomfortable may be their short term consequences. . . . Generally speaking, the Government weighs up carefully the arguments for and against an act of interventionism in any sector of our economy and on the demand or supply side in the light of present and future circumstances. The Government then comes to a positive decision as to where the balance of advantage lies.

On closer reading, that passage is hopelessly vague. But it was presumably interpreted as the green light for the continuing interventionist leanings of Tung Chee Hwa's term as chief executive. However, as time passed, while he still harped on about the overall need for restructuring, the focus of the presumed restructuring requirements began to shift. The somewhat futuristic emphasis on technological advancement gave way to emphasis on more immediate activities. His January 2003 address, as foreshadowed by the new financial secretary, Antony Leung, in his 2002 budget speech, spoke of the need to reinforce the four existing pillars of the economy — finance, logistics, tourism, and professional and producer services. Interestingly, Leung had also done some heart-searching over the philosophical justification for activist policies, including "considering the need to take appropriate measures to secure projects beneficial to our economy as a whole when the private sector is not ready to invest in them".

The emphasis on four key sectors persisted through Tung's last two addresses in October 2004 and January 2005. Noteworthy were various infrastructural initiatives, seen as generally supportive of the logistics sector — improved road and rail links with the Mainland, including the study of a bridge to link Hong Kong with Macau and Zhuhai — and several new tourist-based initiatives — the Lantau cable car, a wetland park, improvements to the Peak and to the Tsim Sha Tsui and Stanley waterfronts. But the ambition to excel and lead in the high-tech zone was still present, with pronouncements of support for the application of technologies which would promote the knowledge-based economy. And there was continued mention of support for cultural and creative industries, with the (proposed) establishment of a Digital Media Centre, an i-resource centre and a design centre — the last to be supported by a grant for a 'design smart' initiative.

While on the subject of culture, it was back in 1998 that Tung Chee Hwa first talked of building a major cultural complex in West Kowloon. The controversial architectural design of a canopy roof, and the decision to put the project to tender on the basis that a single developer would be awarded the entire massive project, again ignited the sort of debate which earlier raged over Cyberport and Disneyland. Growing opposition from the Legislative Council and property developers, and scepticism of the general public, have since led the government to rethink the whole project, and its future hangs in the balance.

Further evidence of the administration's predilection for grandiose gestures comes from Hong Kong's successful lobbying to stage the equestrian events of the 2008 Beijing Olympic Games. The announcement by the secretary for home affairs included the following:

> Hong Kong is proud to share the joy and glory of the 2008 Olympic and Paralympic Games . . . enhancing Hong Kong's status as a hub for important sporting events. Hong Kong can also enjoy the economic benefits brought about by horse-lovers who come to Hong Kong for the equestrian events. . . . a once-in-a-life-time opportunity for Hong Kong to showcase the world our charisma. We have the passion to hold big international sporting events, and the vigor to receive guests from all around the world. I believe Hong Kong people can make a good host and hope all of us can join hands to make this a quality and colourful event.[16]

There was no analysis or quantification of the purported economic benefits, still less any assessment of the balance between them and the costs which would be incurred. The government might be disposed to argue that there is no burden at all on the public purse, since the running costs will be met by the Beijing Olympic authorities, while the cost of constructing or modifying local venues will be borne by the Hong Kong Jockey Club.[17] However, given that the Jockey Club finances a range of projects for the benefit of the community, which might otherwise make demands on the government's budget, there is an obvious opportunity cost to the people of Hong Kong in sponsoring the Olympics. The beneficiaries of the Olympics decision are more likely to be construction companies and the like which are awarded the related contracts, and the officials who stand to enjoy the kudos of playing hosts to the world's equestrian elite, than the man in the street.

Restructuring

During his almost eight years as chief executive, Tung appeared forever anxious to please everyone, and he seemed to feel a need always to be seen to be doing something. There was perhaps more exhortation than substance to some of his initiatives. But this was a period when the budgetary position was tight. If it had not been so, one might have seen some rather more explicit financial support for pet projects. But at the end of the day he was forced to accept that glamorous high-tech activities was perhaps not where Hong Kong's comparative advantage lay. Rather, it was the relatively unglamorous world of entrepot trade, with its spin-off to a wide range of services, coupled with a bit of tourism, which kept the economy going. And it was not obvious that these sectors needed much funding or encouragement from government in order to carry on doing what they had been successfully doing for many years past.

But Tung appeared to be obsessed by the spectre of restructuring. In the recession years, a supposed failure to restructure fast enough was seen as a partial explanation for below-trend growth. At other times it was cited as a sort of warning of possible turbulence ahead for certain sectors. At all times it was seen as a major challenge and a possible excuse for activist policies.

Box 3.4   The government's emphasis on restructuring

(Extract from the official *Hong Kong Yearbook* for 2005, Chapter 3, reprinted by permission of the Government of the Hong Kong Special Administrative Region.)

Structural change is nothing new to the Hong Kong economy. The past decades have seen constant changes brought about by the rapid developments in the regional and global economic environment. In the 1950s Hong Kong was a thriving entrepôt but it swiftly remade itself into an important manufacturing base serving the world market in the 1960s and 1970s. It then further diversified and evolved into a regional financial centre and a business-cum-trading hub in the 1980s. It was also quick to recognise the opportunities presented by the opening up of the Mainland economy in the late 1970s and has played the key role of middleman between the Mainland and the rest of the world, channelling trade and investment flows into and out of the Mainland. In addition, by relocating production facilities across the boundary, as well as investing in this major economic hinterland on a large scale, Hong Kong entrepreneurs have helped transform South China into the world's largest and fastest growing 'factory'.

By meeting the challenges of rapid technological change and the increasingly intense competition brought about by globalisation, the Hong Kong economy has been moving up the value-added chain, shifting towards higher value-added services and more knowledge-based activities.

The rising living standards of Hong Kong people over the decades is a clear testament to their capacity to adapt to rapid changes with the support from sound and effective market institutions. Structural change is an ongoing process, especially with ever-expanding globalisation.

In recent years, the Hong Kong economy has continued to explore the advantages in 'leveraging the Mainland and engaging ourselves globally'. For instance, the focus of Hong Kong's trade has gradually shifted from re-exports to supply-chain management and high value-added logistics services, which has resulted in offshore trade flourishing. Hong Kong's financial markets have not only become the major fund-raising channel for Mainland enterprises, they are also playing a facilitating role in helping them upgrade corporate governance, enhance operational efficiency, promote brand names and go global. Hong Kong's professionals are playing an active role in providing professional services to the Mainland economy, both contributing to and gaining substantially from the Mainland's new phase of economic development.

The success of the Hong Kong economy in meeting the challenges and seizing the opportunities arising from structural changes has always depended, and will continue to depend, on its people. A better-educated and more highly skilled workforce is the key to the flexibility and resilience of the economy. Over the past decade, Hong Kong's labour force has been growing at an average annual rate of 1.6 per cent, but the higher-skilled, professional and managerial component of the labour force has been growing at a much faster average annual rate of 4 per cent. Today, one out of three people in Hong Kong's labour force belongs to this vibrant group of workers.

If the administration's emphasis on structural change has been a little less strident under Tung's successor, it certainly still remains on the agenda, as may be seen from the quotation in Box 3.4 from the *Yearbook* for 2005 (written in 2006). However, the quotation does at least confess that structural change is nothing new.

Hong Kong has, indeed, been undergoing structural change for much of its modern history. Substantial economic upheaval and adjustment occurred, for example, in response to developments in China and the various waves of immigration from the Mainland, and as a result of the quite sudden onset of manufacturing decline after Mainland economic reforms had begun in the late 1970s to bring it into serious contention as a competitor. What is at issue today is whether the government is right to try to predict the economic direction in which such events may steer Hong Kong.

Not conspicuously successful

On balance, past attempts to direct the course of the economy have not been particularly successful.

Since the 1970s, on the subsidised industrial estates, despite their being quite fully tenanted, the type of industry and activity, though modern and state-of-the-art, has scarcely been pushing the frontiers of new technology in the way originally envisaged.

Corresponding efforts during Tung Chee Hwa's period as chief executive to boost the science and technology sector have resulted in a fair amount of disappointment. Cyberport, a science park, an applied science and technology research institute,[18] a second industrial technology centre, and a $5 billion Innovation and Technology Fund were all established, but their benefits seem to have been disproportionately meagre relative to the amounts of investment. Nor have the initiatives to develop Hong Kong into a centre for Chinese medicine — trumpeted in the 1997 and 1998 policy addresses — made a very strong impact. And the film industry, which should have benefited from the 1997 plan to set up the Film Services Advisory Committee and the 1998 decision to establish a $100 million Film Development Fund, has shown little sign of sustained revival.

As noted by two respected academics in 2004:

> [it is] early days to evaluate whether initiatives [such as ASTRI, ITF, Chinese medicine centre, science park & design centre] will bear fruit. . . . but it is clear that such an approach will invite rent-seeking behaviour that is difficult to guard against . . . Hong Kong has inherited a peculiar governance structure that borders on being dysfunctional. . . . Arguably, the most important thing for Hong Kong's future prosperity is to reform its public governance structure by making it more responsive to public interest, rather than being worn down by special interests. . . . A focused minimalist approach [to intervention] is the best way forward.[19]

The role played by the special interests referred to here is examined more closely later.

On the other hand, the initiatives aimed at enhancing Hong Kong as a regional hub and facilitating the flow of goods and peoples across the border with the Mainland — notably the Closer Economic Partnership Arrangement with the Mainland — are perhaps the only ones that could be regarded as definite successes.

Closer Economic Partnership Arrangement

If the government's urge to plan the economy has diminished somewhat compared with the Tung Chee Hwa era, the reason may lie with personalities, but it may also be because of the mounting emphasis on Mainland opportunities and the realisation that Hong Kong, provided that it remains flexible on the supply side and retains its attraction as a place for doing business, should be able to slip-stream the buoyant Mainland economy. If that is accepted, then there is perhaps no longer the need, which was perceived at certain times in the past, to provide targeted support for particular sectors or activities.

In the context of its economic relations with the Mainland, the Closer Economic Partnership Arrangement between Hong Kong and the Mainland (CEPA) has been a major achievement for Hong Kong. The Hong Kong administration had realised that Hong Kong could, and must, prosper from the rapid growth of the Mainland economy. In order to enhance that benefit, it successfully negotiated reductions in trade barriers and increased market access which will give Hong Kong a head start over other competitors who, generally speaking, will eventually gain similar access when China opens its markets more generally under its WTO obligations.

Box 3.5   The Closer Economic Partnership Arrangement*

Technically, CEPA is a bilateral Free Trade Agreement under terms permitted by the World Trade Organisation. It enables Hong Kong to interlock more firmly with the mainland, and smaller Hong Kong businesses in particular to expand their business with the mainland, before the mainland opens its doors more widely.

Under stage I of CEPA, which took effect from 1 January 2004, some 90% of Hong Kong domestic exports to the mainland enjoyed zero tariffs; and mainland access was granted, in varying degrees, to Hong Kong companies in 18 service industries. Companies with substantive activity in Hong Kong (and having been operating there for at least 3–5 years), even if foreign, qualify as Hong Kong companies for the entitlement of these benefits. In addition, the relevant professional and regulatory bodies of Hong Kong and the mainland have concluded various agreements or arrangements for mutual recognition of professional qualifications. The mainland authorities also agreed to progressively expand the facility for mainlanders for make visits to Hong Kong as individuals (rather than being restricted to groups), and to allow mainland enterprises to invest more easily in Hong Kong.

Under stage II, mostly effective from 1 January 2005, the coverage of tariff-free trade was widened further, conditions of access to the Mainland market were enhanced for 11 of the 18 service sectors already covered by stage I, and a further 8 areas of services were liberalised.

Under stage III, effective from 1 January 2006, the export of all products satisfying criteria of Hong Kong origin (other than prohibited articles) became tariff free for import to the mainland, and there was a further batch of liberalisation measures in service sectors, including a few which went further than obligations under the WTO would require.

From 1 July 2006, more Hong Kong products were added to the list of those admitted tariff-free to the mainland. And a further 15 liberalisation measures affecting 10 sectors were scheduled for 1 January 2007.

* (Fuller details of CEPA can be found on the web site of the Hong Kong Trade Development Council, www.cepa.tdctrade.com.)

Other initiatives are being pursued to expand economic ties within the Pearl River Delta region and somewhat further afield, such as through the Pan-Pearl River Delta Regional Development and Co-operation Forum, formed in 2003 — although that particular forum is perhaps more notable for the length of its title and its penchant for conferences than for any concrete achievements to date.

Hong Kong retains many advantages over the Mainland as a well-regulated, transparent, largely corruption-free business environment, with a well-established common law system, clear property rights, sound financial system, and so on. It markets itself, therefore, as the business centre for China, but always in the knowledge that China itself is trying hard to catch up and remedy its deficiencies — something which may, however, take many years.

Back to the supply side . . . ?

Donald Tsang's first policy address as chief executive in October 2005 was a significant contrast to Tung, in that he resisted any temptation to single out particular sectors for favourable mention, despite he himself, while financial secretary, having been very much the earlier champion of initiatives such as Cyberport, Disneyland and, while chief secretary for administration, the west Kowloon cultural complex. Rather, his visible economic emphasis has been more on the supply side, such as improving education, while leaving businesses to exploit the various opportunities presented by market-opening regional initiatives, notably CEPA and the individual Mainland travellers scheme.

This hint of a shift of official attitude has also been evident in the budgets of Financial Secretary Henry Tang since 2004. Adopting as his slogan "The market leads; government facilitates", he has eschewed any major new initiatives to pander to particular sectors with handouts. He has, however, kept alive some of the initiatives of his predecessors, such as support to tourism and transport infrastructure, and, somewhat curiously, to fashion design and the film industry. He has mostly resisted the temptation to spout visionary waffle of the type which used to pad out some of his predecessors' budget speeches. Modest measures to make the business environment more user-friendly and to broaden the minds of students are encouraging signs in the right direction of an underlying 'supply-side' ethos, which is a welcome re-affirmation of Hong Kong's long-held economic philosophy.[20] In sum, Tang's budgets have tended to be shorter, rather duller, but nevertheless sufficient for the purpose.

All of this seems to be somewhat in contrast with the Tung Chee Hwa years when Hong Kong seemed to be edging ever closer to a planned economy.

. . . Or still disposed to economic activism?

But, if the role of government is being played down a bit by the present chief executive and financial secretary, this might just be a change of presentation more than of substance. The government's penchant to interfere has not evaporated completely.

One illustration of this can be found in the case of the proposed Lantau Logistics Park. The secretary for economic development and labour, Stephen Ip, explained it in the following terms to the Legislative Council (1 June 2005):[21]

> The consultancy study . . . completed in September 2001, identified the development of logistics parks as one of the key initiatives to maintain

and enhance Hong Kong's logistics competitiveness. . . . The Scoping Study on the Lantau Logistics Park, completed in August 2004, further confirmed the demand for logistics space in Hong Kong. . . . It is an important infrastructure to promote service integration, and enable logistics enterprises to enjoy economies of scale. It will enhance the overall competitiveness of Hong Kong's logistics industry, which accounts for over 5% of our GDP and provides about 200,000 jobs for the local labour force.

The proposal in effect follows the well-tried formula of granting land to a particular sector at sub-market prices. The extent of subsidy is hard to gauge, because part of it amounts to revenue foregone (compared to the alternative of selling the land for other usage), and part of it is subsumed in public infrastructure projects of which the Park will not necessarily be the sole beneficiary, but which might not be undertaken were it not for the Park.

A hint of a possibly more wide-ranging interventionist tendency also arose when, as noted earlier, the Mainland government mentioned Hong Kong for the first time in its five-year plan in 2006. Hong Kong's chief executive, Donald Tsang, then appeared to feel obliged to be seen to be doing something in response; or perhaps he saw it as an opportunity to make obeisance to Beijing. Whatever the reason, he immediately scheduled a 'summit' for September 2006, stating that

> We must act right now to harness the strong momentum from the mainland to drive our own development, to improve the lives and earning capacity of the general public and to make our unique contribution to the modernisation of the country. . . . The summit will be a pragmatic discussion forum.[22]

The summit spawned four sectoral focus groups, covering trade and business; financial services; innovation and technology; and tourism.[23] Their ensuing deliberations were drawn together into an 'action agenda', which Tsang presented in January 2007.[24] In the event, the action agenda allayed any fears there might have been about a possible escalation of formal economic planning. It proposed a lot of further study, along with a series of measures which, if implemented, would remove barriers to business; improve or streamline regulation; and expand market access in both directions across the border, and on many fronts — trade, finance, transport, professional services, and so on.

Progress on this agenda will be heavily dependent upon help from the Mainland. In this context it may be remarked that Hong Kong is in a somewhat ambivalent position. It seeks, when it suits, to be treated as just another Chinese city, and feels that, as a Chinese insider, it should play a part in moulding the Mainland's agenda for economic and financial reform. At the same time, however, Hong Kong likes to emphasise to the world at large that it is economically separate under its 'one country, two systems' constitutional status. In its quest to expand business with the Mainland, Hong Kong must take care not to dilute any of its own business standards in a way which might dent its appeal to the wider world.

In one sense, the Hong Kong government's enthusiastic response to the Mainland's planning initiative can be regarded as a pragmatic engagement, seizing the opportunity to play some part in Mainland policies which will inevitably have a bearing on Hong Kong, even if only indirectly, and thereby being better placed to anticipate Hong Kong's future infrastructural needs.

In another sense, however, the Hong Kong government's response might signal too great a readiness to allow the Mainland to fashion Hong Kong's own development,[25] as well as providing a pretext for the Hong Kong government to micro-manage the economy. Then, taking account also of the mindset behind the relaunch of the Commission on Strategic Development (see Chapter 7), one could be forgiven for wondering whether Hong Kong's present leader might not be just as dirigiste as was his predecessor.

– 4 –

The Budget and Public Finances

Overview

The scale of a government's budget and the nature of its actual expenditures provide a guide, albeit a qualified one, to the scale of its involvement in the economy.

Despite fiscal deficits for most of the period from 1998 to 2005, Hong Kong is one of very few economies, and one of even fewer economies of significant size, where the government has had a tradition of budget surpluses, and so has accumulated fiscal reserves rather than debt. As at the end of the fiscal year 2005–06 the fiscal reserve, which embraces both the accumulation of past surpluses (net of deficits) and investment earnings on them, amounted to $311 billion, equivalent to 23% of annual GDP, whereas government borrowing stood at only $25 billion (1.8% of GDP). Provisional figures for the 2006–07 fiscal year put the reserves at $369 billion and debt at $22 billion. The reserves would be larger still, were it not for the deficits of the 1998–2005 period.

Hong Kong's budget deficit reached almost 5% of GDP in 2001–02 and 2002–03, in the aftermath of the 1997 Asian financial turmoil and the resulting recession in Hong Kong, which was exacerbated by the SARS crisis of 2003, and by the bursting of the property bubble which had reached a peak in 1997 and left the market in the doldrums for a few years. By 2005–6 the budget had swung back into surplus, without resort to any very stringent tax increases, but helped by a cyclical upswing in revenue from land sales and by successful economies in public spending. This return to surplus was in apparent defiance of predictions that a fundamental adverse structural shift had occurred in public finances.

Table 4.1 Budget statistics

| Economy | Average for the five years 2002–06 (latest year estimated) as percentage of gross domestic product | |
	Fiscal balance (general government)	Gross government debt (end-years)
United States	-4.0	61.7
Euro area (combined)	-2.5	69.5
Japan	-6.7	173.8
United Kingdom	-2.9	40.7
Hong Kong	-0.9	1.1

Source: IMF *World Economic Outlook,* September 2006, and Hong Kong Treasury.

| Hong Kong: Consolidated annual budget balance | |
financial year to 31 March	HK$ billion
1997	+25.8
1998	+86.9#
1999	-23.2
2000	+10.0
2001	-7.8
2002	-63.3
2003	-61.7
2004	-40.1
2005	-4.0★
2006	+14.0
2007	+58.6△

\# Includes $43.5 billion of land-related revenues from earlier years previously held in suspense.
★ Before taking into account the proceeds of issuance of bonds and notes totalling $23.4 billion.
△ Provisional: Government press release, 30 April 2007.
Source: Government Treasury and *Hong Kong Annual Review.*

Hong Kong's strong fiscal position has been the result of long-standing budgetary conservatism established during the British colonial era. The build-up of budget surpluses reflected a mixture of a quasi-mercantilist desire to accumulate, a belief that deficits were intrinsically bad, and a tendency to err on the side of caution. More fundamentally, the trend reflected the fact that the government was in most respects a reluctant spender — in particular eschewing the tendency of many Western economies to allow ballooning social policy budgets. This is illustrated by the figures for government spending in Table 4.2, where Hong Kong and Singapore appear to be in a league of their own.

Table 4.3 shows how, within the total of public spending, the proportion devoted to social welfare is lower than in most developed economies, reflecting traditional reliance on self-help and family support, and a distaste for the

Table 4.2 Selected economies: Government spending

Country	Government spending as percentage of GDP
Australia	36
Austria	49
Belgium	49
Canada	39
China	32
Denmark	54
Finland	51
France	54
Germany	47
Hong Kong	**20★**
Ireland	36
Italy	49
Japan	37
Luxembourg	46
Netherlands	48
New Zealand	38
Norway	46
Portugal	48
Singapore	16
Spain	38
Sweden	57
Switzerland	37
United Kingdom	45
United States	37

Sources: For member countries of the Organisation for Economic Cooperation and Development, *OECD Economic Outlook*. For Hong Kong, annex to budget speech. For China, OECD estimates reported in *OECD Observer*, no. 251, September 2005; this estimate is probably closest to being on the same basis as other OECD figures in the table; alternative estimates from the IMF yield a figure of only 21%, but this excludes local government outlays and social security (IMF public information notice, PIN 05/122 of September 2005). For Singapore, Statistics Singapore at www.singstat.gov.sg. All figures are estimates for 2005 of total general government outlays as a percentage of gross domestic product.

★ Forecast to fall to 17.4% by 2007–08 according to government budget projections of February 2007.

dependency culture and presumptions of state support that are prevalent especially in some European economies. The slice of resources going to housing has been declining, but there is still a significant element of subsidy to public housing tenants.

The share of spending in the 'economic' category reflects *inter alia* support for particular sectors. Although this is a fairly modest number, two factors should be borne in mind. First, much assistance has been given by providing land at sub-market prices; this does not get recorded as an expenditure item. Second, some spending which is classified as being for infrastructure may in fact be a disguised subsidy to a particular sector.

Table 4.3   Hong Kong: Composition of public expenditure*
(percentages of total spending)

Policy area	Share
Education	21.4
Social welfare	14.0
Health	12.2
Security	10.8
Infrastructure	8.4
Housing	5.9
Economic	5.8
Environment and food	4.4
Community and external affairs	3.2
Support (e.g. central administration)	14.0

* Official estimates for 2007–08 from *The Budget, 2007–08.*

The Basic Law

The most important formal parameter governing fiscal policy is the Basic Law, which states (Article 107) that Hong Kong shall "strive to achieve a fiscal balance, avoid deficits and keep the budget commensurate with the growth rate of its gross domestic product". Use of the word "strive", rather than something more imperative, is suggestive of a certain flexibility. Would it, for example, be permissible to miss the targets provided that a sufficient effort had been made? Perhaps so in the short term, but to do so indefinitely would make a mockery of the Basic Law. Thus, although there is no reference to any time horizon, it is generally presumed that the Law allows flexibility over the economic cycle, but not indefinitely. The Hong Kong government itself has kept very quiet over the question of interpretation of this part of the Basic Law, probably because, wisely, it would like to retain the maximum flexibility that the wording could be construed to allow.

Well before the Basic Law came into effect, the Hong Kong government had, over the years, evolved a number of informal rules on budgetary practice, which became a sort of folklore, but which have in recent years become subject to some fairly radical adjustment in response to changing circumstances.

The fiscal reserve

The first rule of thumb relates to a desire to maintain a fiscal reserve: that is, the unspent accumulated funds from past budget surpluses. These are held in the government's Exchange Fund and invested in a manner which ensures a high degree of liquidity. In 2002, the then financial secretary indicated that:

> In my view, it should be sufficient to have fiscal reserves equivalent to around 12 months of government expenditure to meet operating and contingency requirements.[26]

Budget addresses in the intervening years have given the clear impression that 12 months' cover was as low a figure as should be tolerated. By the start of the fiscal year 2007–08 the cover had risen to about 19 months, and, in his February 2007 budget speech, the financial secretary suggested that a range of 30–50% of GDP could be used as a "frame of reference" — equivalent to 18 to 24 months' cover of government expenditure. Then he added, referring to some IMF calculations, that a further 18 months' worth might need to be set aside by the year 2030 as a cushion against the burden of an ageing population.

Historically, as implied by the above quotation, the fiscal reserve has been regarded essentially as a liquidity management tool, to ensure that at all times there are enough funds immediately available to cover government outgoings and any unforeseen contingencies. In that respect, it is simply a facet of cash management and should not command a lot of headline attention. It has also been regarded, however, as a symbol of financial virility since, for most of the time, the reserve represented both the gross and the net financial wealth of the government in simple budgetary terms.

Now that the government has, in recent years, done some borrowing, its net wealth has to be gauged by netting off the borrowing from the reserves. But borrowing remains extremely modest. The Hong Kong government still has positive net fiscal assets amounting to over 25% of GDP and this figure is currently on the rise. The net position of most other economies is persistently negative, being dominated by large levels of government debt outstanding. In the run-up to monetary union, the countries of what is now the euro area were required to reduce their government debt to what was regarded as a safe and sustainable level (or to demonstrate substantive progress in that direction). In that context, anything up to 60% of GDP was considered safe. Application of this criterion to Hong Kong would permit government *borrowing* of up to about HK$850 billion. This compares with the government's belief (at least until recently, see below) that borrowing should, if at all possible, be avoided altogether, and that safety means *reserves* of at least about HK$300 billion. From a Hong Kong perspective, the difference between these two yardsticks for prudent fiscal policy amounts to well in excess of one trillion HK dollars.

One might be tempted to conclude that the government is excessively conservative in this domain. However, the financial secretary's reference to an ageing population serves as a reminder of the budgetary pressures which could mount in future — not least because, for instance, public sector pensions are unfunded and have therefore to be financed by the government as they fall due. Even so, most governments around the world are net debtors in the financial markets, rather than net asset holders.

An oft-heard, additional argument for maintaining substantial fiscal reserves is that they also represent part of Hong Kong's foreign exchange reserves. However, as will be discussed in Chapter 5, the reasoning commonly deployed by officials about the linkage between fiscal and foreign exchange reserves is basically fallacious.

An operating surplus

The second long-standing rule of thumb is that the budget should always display a surplus of recurrent revenue over recurrent expenditure,[27] in order to make a contribution to the financing of capital expenditure (i.e. to fund that part of capital spending which is not covered by what are defined as capital revenues, such as land premiums and asset sales).

This rule fits the conservative tradition that indebtedness is bad. If the fiscal reserve is to be protected and if borrowing is to be avoided, then capital expenditure, notably on infrastructure, has to be funded from revenue of some sort. Since capital revenue is often insufficient, a surplus must be earned on recurrent account to fill the gap.

By way of comparison, the fiscal rule for countries in the euro area is that overall budget deficits should not exceed 3% of GDP. The UK rule is that the current account component should not be in deficit; this implies that it would be considered imprudent to run down financial wealth or incur debts simply to fund items of current expenditure. But by the same token it would be perfectly permissible to fund capital spending through running down assets or by borrowing, because the capital expenditure would itself be creating an asset to replace the one being used up to finance it. It would anyway be presumed that a cost-benefit analysis had been conducted to ascertain that this switch within the balance sheet — increasing physical capital at the cost of reducing net financial capital — was indeed likely to benefit society in the broadest public policy sense.

Even the UK rule, however, is a simplification of a complex issue. Any policy position involves crucially considerations of intergenerational equity. Strict equity would dictate that the optimal strategy is indeed to keep the current account in balance, since then society which is paying tax today is receiving an exactly matched benefit in the form of today's current government expenditure. It is argued that the running of a current surplus would be unfair to the present generation, since part of the taxes they paid would be going either towards capital projects or simply into government coffers, from either of which only the future generation would benefit. On the other hand, to run a current deficit would be profligate in imposing a burden on future generations, because today's government would either be squandering assets or incurring debts which would have to be repaid in the future.

That argument may itself, however, need to be qualified. It could be claimed, in one direction, that because of the problems of an ageing population and because people cannot be counted upon to save enough for themselves, the state should assume a relatively greater burden of social support in future. This would, in turn, justify taxing people a bit more today and so running a current budget surplus. On the other hand, it may be argued that, if one is reasonably confident that the economy will continue to grow, thereby yielding improvements in *per capita* real incomes and living standards, then tomorrow's generation will be capable of looking after tomorrow's pensioners, and there is therefore no need to tax today's generation, which is poorer than tomorrow's will be, in order to look after them.

There are, therefore, many diverse considerations to be taken into account when developing fiscal rules. It is unclear whether the Hong Kong government has ever comprehensively assessed these issues. It is even less clear whether the rules of thumb that have been followed have been appropriate.

Government borrowing

The third plank of the government's fiscal creed was, for many years a strong aversion to government borrowing. In practice the government has issued small amounts of debt for budgetary purposes, but only on a few occasions (see Box 4.1). Officials were perpetually wary of indebtedness, and would cite *inter alia* the concern that international rating agencies might downgrade Hong Kong as a result. However, if that concern was justified, it was a dilemma largely of successive governments' own making. Over the years Hong Kong had persistently boasted about the virtue of the government not borrowing (albeit without any very convincing economic analysis to substantiate the claim), implying by corollary that to borrow would indeed be bad for Hong Kong.

Box 4.1   Government borrowing

The government issued relatively small amounts of bonds, of fairly short maturities (typically 2–3 years), in the periods 1975–76, 1984–85, and 1991–93. In each case the purpose was to help fund capital projects — the new airport in the last instance, although it transpired that the budget could have anyway covered the amounts without lapsing into deficit.

In May 2004, Toll Revenue Bonds were issued, which were secured on tolls receivable from government tolled tunnels and bridges. The issue totalled $6 billion, with tranches of one, three and five-year maturities.

In July 2004 the government made a further issue, of notes and bonds totalling $20 billion. These comprised institutional notes of HK$5 billion and retail bonds of HK$5.25 billion denominated in Hong Kong dollars, as well as institutional notes of US$1.25 billion denominated in US dollars. Maturities ranged from two months to eight years.

Meanwhile, the government's Exchange Fund began issuing short-term bills of up to one year's maturity in March 1990 and notes of longer maturities — eventually as long as ten years — in May 1993. This programme was, however, designed to assist the Monetary Authority in its management of the money market, and banks in the management of their liquidity, as well as to foster development of the local debt market. It has not been used to fund the government's budget and has played no direct part in that process.

One could not therefore have complained if the rating agencies swallowed that line and downgraded Hong Kong when the government began to borrow, even though those same agencies have scarcely batted an eyelid at the massive public debts of several other economies which have remained highly rated. A managed strategy of debt finance is a feature of virtually every successful business; why should a successful government not likewise indulge? In the event, the agencies were not unduly aroused by the Hong Kong government's decision to resume borrowing in 2004; indeed Hong Kong received upgrades from the agencies in that and the following years.

This sequence of events lends support to the view that the government ought not to set itself against borrowing, or be embarrassed when forced into it. Nevertheless, there probably remain some people, both in government and in the business world, who regard the decision to borrow as a highly retrograde step, representing a collapse of discipline, a sign of weakness, and so on.

A particular weakness in the official line on this issue over many years was a failure to realise that, in financial terms, there is little difference between running down one's assets (i.e. the fiscal reserves) and borrowing. Both actions deplete financial net worth. Successive governments appear, on balance, to have been even more protective of their 'safe' level of reserves than of their debt-free status. In fact, the choice between the two is primarily a judgement of strategic portfolio management and liquidity considerations. They cannot be regarded as intrinsically different in principle.

What to do with the rules

In fact, the 'rule' about having an operating surplus has been broken in some recent years as a result of sub-trend economic growth in 1998 and again in the period 2001–03. The operating account returned to surplus in 2005–06 (Table 4.4), while the capital account was roughly in balance, supported by buoyant land premiums (which are usually the predominant component of capital revenue). On this occasion, therefore, the operating surplus did not have to be used to help cover capital spending; an overall (consolidated) surplus emerged, which could be added to the fiscal reserve. Provisional figures for 2006–07 indicate substantial surpluses on both operating account and capital account.

Table 4.4   Government financing, 2005–06

operating account		$ billion
operating revenue	196.5	
operating expenditure	192.5	
surplus before investment income		**4.0**
investment income	8.1	
surplus after investment income		**12.1**
capital financing		
capital revenue, including asset sales	40.2	
capital spending	39.8	
investment income less interest expenses	1.4	
surplus		**1.8**
consolidated surplus		**14.0**

Source: Hong Kong Treasury web site, reprinted by permission of the Government of the Hong Kong Special Administrative Region.

A particular criticism of the rules arises from the treatment of land-related revenue. Because land is a fixed asset and land premiums are in effect paid by developers in order to acquire that asset for a long, albeit not an indefinite, period, the premium income has always been logged as capital revenue. This should not normally, according to the self-imposed rules, be used to finance items of current (or 'operating') expenditure. Rather the reverse: surpluses on operating account have been encouraged or required in order to help finance capital spending.

There is, however, a respectable argument that, since the government continually creates new land for sale, and is continually renewing leases or exacting payments for changes in use, its land-related income bears all the characteristics of recurrent revenue. If it were to be taken into the operating account rather than the capital account, it would permit a significantly higher level of expenditure on current items, such as health and welfare. As the system stands, the critics would argue, it is biased towards capital spending, which explains why Hong Kong has, for example, a first-class transport infrastructure but a second-class system of social support for the poor.

However, the biggest inconvenience, or possible danger, for Hong Kong in the fiscal arena lies not so much in having to adapt continuously its own rules of thumb — which can be done with no more than a passing embarrassment for any financial secretary who finds himself eating his words — as from the Basic Law provisions, if they are to be taken seriously. For instance, the edict that the budget must balance appears to exclude the very sensible option of funding capital projects, even if strongly supported by cost-benefit analysis, through drawing on reserves or borrowing on the capital market.[28] And, by limiting the growth of the budget (which presumably refers to the gross level of revenues and expenditures) to the growth rate of the economy, the Basic Law appears to rule out the rise in spending relative to GDP which many regard as essential to match society's loftier aspirations for social support, health, education, and so forth.

In sum, none of the rules — either the formal or the informal — has any rigorous economic foundation. Rather, they are fairly general expressions of financial prudence as popularly perceived, and they provide a safeguard against plainly irresponsible budgetary policies. In economic terms, factors such as the social rate of return on public investment relative to the opportunity cost of the necessary funding, and considerations of intergenerational equity, should play a central role in budgetary decisions. But there is little evidence of such factors being systematically embedded in the budget process. For as long as the government's hands are tied by the Basic Law, and by other rules which lack a rigorous economic foundation, its fiscal decisions are unlikely to deliver an optimal allocation of resources. That is an unintended and adverse consequence of policies that have been devised with the best of 'hands-off' intentions at heart.

Accrual accounts

In recent years the official budgetary arithmetic has been subject to a new initiative in accrual accounting. This is highly significant, and may in due course be seen to justify a revision to some of the rules which have been embedded up to now in the fiscal process. Accrual accounting, when applied, brings the government's accounts much closer in conformity to those of commercial companies in the private sector. However, full congruence is perhaps neither possible nor desirable, given that a government is involved in certain activities which other entities seldom indulge in, and carries assets and liabilities which few private entities would have on their balance sheets. The main differences between the new accrual accounts and Hong Kong's traditional cash accounting are listed in Box 4.2.

Box 4.2   Two approaches to government accounting

Main differences between the accrual accounts and Hong Kong's traditional cash accounting

In the **income-expenditure account**

(a) the accrual accounts take notice of the entire surpluses of the Exchange Fund (i.e. consolidating the Fund's surplus fully into the government accounts) whereas the cash accounts only recognise the share of surpluses which is apportionable to the fiscal reserve;

(b) the accrual accounts allow for depreciation of fixed assets and for provisions (e.g. for amounts owed which may not be repaid), whereas the cash accounts do not;

(c) the accrual accounts disregard proceeds from payments to acquire, or proceeds from sales of, fixed assets, and cash flows from purely financing transactions such as issuance of government bonds and notes, since these result in no change to the government's net assets, whereas the cash accounts recognise the cash flows.

In terms of the **balance sheet**, the accrual accounts provide a much broader view of the government's net asset position than does the mere fiscal reserve (which has traditionally been the focus of attention). They take on board all the assets of the Exchange Fund, net of the government's liabilities arising from issuance of bonds and notes, but also recognise the substantial future liability which the government carries in respect of public sector pensions. In fact, this last item predominates, with the result that the net asset position is somewhat weaker than that described by the fiscal reserve alone.

Best endeavours by the Hong Kong Treasury to apply accrual accounting in a meaningful way to the accounts of the government have revealed, for three of the four years for which the comparisons are available, a generally stronger fiscal performance in terms of the annual surplus or deficit than displayed in the conventional framework. But the balance sheet emerges as weaker, with the future liability to pay civil servant pensions outweighing the benefit from taking all of the Exchange Fund's assets into account. The differences are summarised in Table 4.5.

Table 4.5 Budget accounting comparisons (HK$ billion)

	year to 31 March 2003	year to 31 March 2004	year to 31 March 2005	year to 31 March 2006
cash basis consolidated account				
surplus/deficit for year	deficit 61.7	deficit 40.1	surplus 21.4	surplus 14.0
fiscal reserve, end-year (net assets)	315.5	275.3	296.0	310.7
accrual-based statement of financial performance				
surplus/deficit for year	deficit 43.4	surplus 11.0	surplus 19.4	surplus 47.6
general reserve, end-year (net assets)	217.5	155.9	152.4	185.5

Source: Hong Kong Treasury web site, reprinted by permission of the Government of the Hong Kong Special Administrative Region.

In addition to the accounting review which led to the compilation of accrual accounts, the government has conducted two other important reviews of budgetary issues in recent years. These are considered in the next two sections.

Task Force on Review of Public Finances

This task force, which reported in February 2002, tackled the question of whether the budget deficit, looming at the time, represented merely a cyclical phenomenon, or was symptomatic of an underlying structural deficit. The report concluded that

> Hong Kong is facing a persistent fiscal problem. Some of the forces leading to this situation are believed to be structural in nature . . . findings [from economic simulations] show unequivocal signs that even when the economy returns to 'normal' the budget deficits will remain and indeed worsen.

This view was based on the reasoning that, as the economy grows and, with it, the public's expectations of the quality and range of public services, there would be strong upward pressure on public spending (in other developed economies it tends to rise as a proportion of GDP, and stands at a considerably higher proportion than in Hong Kong). In order to keep the overall budgetary balance within limits (i.e. prevent any deficit, or at least any excessive one), the report recommended that priority be given to containing expenditure. Failing that, revenue would have to be increased. But traditional revenue sources might not be relied upon. The report raised concerns that revenue from land sales, which had been a mainstay in the past, might tail off; betting duty was already having to be restructured in the hope of arresting the declining trend from that source; and Hong Kong's territorial-based system of profits tax and salaries tax might result in a shrinking tax base, since only profits and salaries sourced in Hong Kong are taxed — which encouraged taxpayers to present a picture to the authorities which minimised such sourcing. So, if higher marginal tax rates on profits or salaries were to be avoided, either more people would have to be brought into the tax net or, if it was not considered wise or practicable to raise sufficient additional revenue from existing taxes, then new taxes might need to be introduced.

In retrospect, this report was too bearish about property-based revenue. The authors seemed to overlook the fact that the government's monopoly on land supply could still, if desired, be adequately exploited to generate good revenues, so long as Hong Kong retained its wider attractions as a place to locate and reside. The report also seemed to overlook the fact that, in view of Hong Kong's low rates of taxation, people might, unless they could manage to escape tax in every possible jurisdiction, prefer to present profits and salaries as being sourced in low-tax Hong Kong than in other places. Finally, the report perhaps gave insufficient consideration to the constraint which the Basic Law might impose on spending.

Advisory Committee on New Broad-based Taxes

In parallel with the above Task Force, this committee explored the options for new taxes which might be needed if the conclusions of the Task Force were accepted. The committee reported in 2002, concluding that, of all the options, a goods and service tax was best suited as a long-term solution, if one was needed.

Efficiency in taxation

In keeping with its 'hands-off' image, Hong Kong rightly prides itself in maintaining a low tax environment. Corporate profits — but only those arising from activity in Hong Kong — are taxed at 17.5%. Salaries tax is the only component of personal income which is subject to tax, and it cannot exceed 16% of an individual's salary. Investment income is not taxed. There is, to date, no general sales tax. Other sources of revenue include property rates, indirect taxes (such as those on alcohol and tobacco, petrol and betting, the airport departure tax, and stamp duties) and, most importantly, land premiums.

The low tax environment, and especially the fact that not only the average but also the marginal rates on salaries and profits are low, is crucial in sustaining Hong Kong's image as a business-friendly place where government interferes as little as possible in the process of resource allocation, such as the choices between work and leisure, or spending and saving.

However, the system is not entirely free of allocative distortions. The principal one occurs in the realm of land and housing.

Land policy

With a population of seven million and a land area of only about 1,100 square kilometres, Hong Kong is the world's third most densely populated territory, after Macau and Monaco. Less than a quarter of the area is built-up or urbanised, and about half of the remainder is designated as country parks or special areas for the purpose of nature conservation, outdoor recreation and nature education. This means that there is intense pressure of population and activity in the urban areas.

The government owns all the land.[29] It also creates land for development, much of it through reclamation at the waterfront. It retains land for itself, as necessary, for public infrastructure, public housing and so forth, and auctions the rest on long leases for commercial or residential development. Occasionally it gifts land, or sells a lease at a subsidised price, to assist or incentivise certain types of activity (such as industrial estates, science park, transportation systems, schools and hospitals). When seeking renewal of a lease or a change of usage, the lessee is charged a premium based on prevailing market values.

Box 4.3   Villagers' rights: A quaint problem of land policy

Every adult male indigenous villager in the New Territories (one who can trace his village roots back to 1898 when Britain took the lease on the New Territories) can claim the right to be awarded a plot of land at a concessionary price, on which to build a three-storey village house of up to 2,100 square feet in floor area (divisible into flats if desired). Those taking advantage of this quaint arrangement, many of whom no longer inhabit their villages, can make a substantial profit, by selling or renting out the property. There is a large backlog of applications, largely because of a shortage of appropriate sites, which irks the applicants. Meanwhile, officials and the public at large (other than the villagers, of course) are increasingly of the view that this anomalous privilege, which was introduced in 1972 as a supposedly temporary measure to help relieve a housing shortage, should have no place in modern-day Hong Kong. There are also aesthetic concerns about the eyesores which have been created in many villages by poor planning of such developments and unimaginative architecture.

The government is thought to be in favour of scrapping the scheme. Back in 1997 it established a working group to review the arrangement, but progress has been glacial, not least because of the political weight of the villagers, voiced in particular through their organisation, the Heung Yee Kuk. A pilot scheme was proposed in March 2006 to permit the rights to be pooled in order to construct higher buildings. Villagers argue that their right is protected by Article 40 of the Basic Law, which states that: "the lawful traditional rights of and interests of the indigenous inhabitants of the New Territories shall be protected". However, it is not clear whether the privilege amounts to a lawful traditional right; the issue has never yet been tested in the courts.

Whatever are the precise administrative arrangements — and these have changed from time to time over the years — the government effectively controls the land market, since it determines how much to supply and sets a reserve price on its sales. The revenue from land sales and redevelopment fees — collectively termed the land premium — has been a key source of government revenue, averaging around 10% of the total, but uneven from year to year.

With demand outstripping supply for much of the time, property prices have tended to rise faster than consumer prices, although in recent years the pattern has become less clear, with a lot of volatility. There has long been something of an unholy alliance between government and developers in support of rising prices. The former likes high prices as a source of revenue, while the latter depend on a rising market to produce capital gains on land banks and work in progress. The government's stated policy on land supply includes "safeguarding public revenue through the policy of not selling land cheap".[30] In order to keep prices rising, supply has to be appropriately managed. The government has been fortified in its instinct to limit the supply by a growing popular opposition to reclamation, or encroachment onto green areas, on environmental grounds.

One benefit of the government's monopoly of land is that the public purse itself can enjoy some of the development gains which arise from the improvements which the government itself makes to the economy's infrastructure. For example, if a new road generally raises property prices in the vicinity, the government is able to recoup the costs of building the road when it next sells new development sites or renegotiates leases on existing sites in the vicinity. This contrasts with the situation in most other economies, where development gains would accrue largely to the private sector and the government would have no automatic increase in revenue to match the bill for the new road.

In similar vein, the Hong Kong government grants the railway corporations the rights to develop buildings around their stations. Much of the railway infrastructure can be financed from the resulting development profits accruing to the corporations, rather than requiring explicit funding from the budget.

Those are arguments which tend to lend support to a regime of high property prices. Yet high prices go hand in hand with restricted supply, and it is by no means clear that the apportionment of land between development and open space is optimal. From a social angle, and even an environmental one, an argument can be made for extra living space and for greater integration of recreational and natural space with living space.

From the economic point of view, if land was in competitive supply, it would be produced and sold at something much closer to its cost (plus normal profits) than is typical in practice. That would bring down property prices to the benefit of those wishing to buy a home or to live in more spacious accommodation. Even in the private sector, homes are physically very small relative to income and other components of living standards, in comparison to most other advanced economies. And lower prices would also reduce business costs.

Although it is widely presumed that revenue would fall if supply was increased, the likely magnitude of any such fall is unclear; it depends on how responsive prices would be to changes in supply. However, if revenue did fall, the hole would have to be plugged from some other source. And the government's ability to harvest development gains arising from infrastructural investment would be weakened. All in all, the government has always believed that people and businesses will generally tolerate high property rentals and prices, in exchange for keeping taxes low on their other spending, income or profits.

The government may well be correct in that belief, since 49.5% of people, according to official statistics for 2005, live in public rental flats or flats which they have purchased under subsidised sale schemes, and are therefore insulated from any pain associated with high prices, while many of those who are already on the property ladder may welcome appreciating values.

However, high prices only serve to exacerbate the task of weaning a large swathe of the population away from dependency on public housing and getting them started on the ladder of home ownership. And they present businesses with ever-rising premises costs, which offset to some extent the attraction of the otherwise low-taxation environment. Beyond that, the perpetuation of high prices ensures that the mass of the population can only ever afford shoebox-sized homes.

Of course, any change of approach to land supply and prices could be extremely contentious. In particular, any sudden reduction in values would impose windfall losses on existing property owners, with possible uncomfortable consequences for banks. The mere hint of any change could equally cause consternation, and there would be a huge danger of 'insider dealing' if any party had advance warning. All of this would create significant practical challenges for policy makers.

Housing policy

The stated objective of the government's housing policy is to maintain a fair and stable operating environment for the private property market by ensuring adequate land supply and provision of an efficient supporting infrastructure, but, beyond that, to minimise its intervention in the private property market. Meanwhile, the stated focus of the subsidised housing policy is to provide assistance to low-income families who cannot afford to purchase or rent in the private housing sector.[31]

Public housing rents are set by law according to a formula which prescribes that the median rent-to-income ratio across all the public housing estates shall not exceed 10%. The government sets a minimum space allocation standard of 5.5 square metres of internal floor area per person; the average for all public rental housing is 11.7 square metres and the average size of a rented public housing unit is around 35 square metres.

In other words, public housing is cheap but cramped. There is believed to be widespread abuse of eligibility criteria. Many tenants could afford to pay more, but may not be well enough off to make the leap to the private housing sector. Attempts over the years to help them with subsidies in one form or another, such as the Home Ownership Scheme, have encountered opposition from the private developers, and have mostly been discontinued.

Meanwhile, because the construction of public housing is not subject to market forces, its location and design can cause frictions. For instance, should public housing be sited in prime locations or only in places where private demand would be low? How spacious should public housing units be? There is no price mechanism by reference to which such questions can be answered.

Strangely, despite its commitment to the principles of a market economy, the government seems in no hurry to alter its basic approach on housing. This is despite quite damning indictments of the status quo from leading academics and others.[32] The theme of most commentaries is that government should extricate itself from such widespread involvement in the provision of housing, first by steering tenants towards purchasing their flats — if necessary by selling public units at heavily discounted prices — from which a market in lower-cost flats could begin to develop; and, second, by moving to a system whereby, instead of a subsidised rent, people truly in need of social support received an income supplement from the public purse, which would be sufficient for the poorest to maintain their standard of living by renting a home and might enable the somewhat better-off to consider purchasing one. Tenants would, of course, be better able to contemplate such a move if the government was also to climb down from its policy of sustaining high land prices.

Goods and services tax

The prognosis from the Task Force report in 2002 about a persistent deficit may have been unduly pessimistic. Nevertheless, the government, as a long-term insurance against the possibilities of burgeoning social spending or plummeting land revenues, launched an initiative to broaden the tax base by means of a value-added tax, or 'goods and service tax' as it is officially termed. Such a tax would place Hong Kong in line with some 120 other countries.

Accordingly, after much delay, the government issued a discussion paper on GST in July 2006.[33] The paper outlined a plan for a GST set at 5%, which would yield an estimated $30 billion a year. For at least the first five years the proceeds would be channelled back to the public, in a manner designed to neutralise the burden at all levels of society (via social support payments to the poor, for example).

The proposal came under widespread attack. Some critics argued, despite the assurances about compensating expenditure, that the tax would be regressive. Others argued that, even if it was not regressive for the first five years, there was a danger of it becoming so thereafter; and that, anyway, if there was a need for tax reform, the opportunity should actually be taken to introduce a greater degree of progressivity, especially at the top end of the income/wealth scale.

There was also opposition from those who doubted the need to expand the tax base, given the strong recovery in revenues in the latest years, and from those who were sceptical of the practicality of a GST in such an open economy as Hong Kong — particularly because of the likely administrative burden on movements across the Mainland border and on entrepot business.

All of the major political parties came out against the tax, and a motion against it was passed in the Legislative Council on 19 October 2006. Although this motion was not binding on the government, the financial secretary eventually conceded, in December, that there was insufficient public support for a GST, so the plan was effectively shelved. However, the government gauged that the public nevertheless accepted the need to broaden the tax base, and therefore continued to invite views on tax reform.

Progressivity

Choices relating to new taxes or increased tax rates hinge to some extent on how skewed the distribution of income is, whether it is judged desirable to level out inequalities, and, if so, whether the tax system should be assigned that task. Hong Kong is in fact deemed to have a wider gulf between rich and poor than most other economies, as illustrated by the Gini coefficients Table 4.6 (the higher the figure, the more skewed is the income distribution).

Table 4.6 Gini coefficient for selected developed economies (lower figures denote more even distribution of income)

	Gini Coefficient	Survey year
Hong Kong	0.525	2001
Australia	0.352	1994
Canada	0.331	1998
France	0.327	1995
Germany	0.283	2000
Japan	0.249	1993
South Korea	0.316	1998
Singapore	0.425	1998
Sweden	0.250	2000
Taiwan	0.326	2000
United Kingdom	0.360	1999
United States	0.408	2000

Sources: The World Bank (2004), Hong Kong Census and Statistics Department (2002) and *Distribution of Income in Taiwan*. Table reproduced from Legislative Council Factsheet FS07/04–05, compiled by the Research and Library Services Division of the Legislative Council Secretariat.
NB: The coefficients are believed to have been calculated prior to any effects of taxation and social security payments.

Table 4.6 refers to incomes before taxation. Do present fiscal arrangements in Hong Kong succeed in flattening out the income distribution at all? This rather depends upon how progressive is the tax system.

Despite salaries tax not exceeding 16% of any person's salary, the so-called middle classes — typified as those who pay salaries tax but are not notably rich — are characterised as being aggrieved at their tax burden. They seem irked since, beneath them, because of the high starting threshold for salaries tax, fewer than half of Hong Kong workers pay any tax at all, while above them there are wealthy people, who are presumed to be recipients of substantial investment income, which also escapes local tax.

Whether the fiscal system as a whole, taking taxes and benefits together, is adjudged fair, depends heavily on two particular aspects.

At the bottom end is the matter of public housing. It is odd that, in a place of Hong Kong's economic status, half the people live in flats the purchase or rental of which involves public subsidy. On the other hand, social security payouts are generally only modest. These, together with the subsidy implicit in public housing, represent the only redistribution to the lower echelons of society.

At the other end sit the rich, whose tax liability may be miniscule in proportion to their income, wealth or consumption. There may, therefore, be a reasonable case for seeking to extract more tax from those most able to pay. The government has, however, focused its tax reform options on indirect taxes, such as GST, which tend, if anything, to be regressive in their burden.

Other revenue ideas

Among other possibilities which have been explored was a departure levy on persons leaving Hong Kong by the land or sea borders. This was first mooted by the financial secretary in his 1999 budget speech. It was to be dressed up as a border facilities development charge and, although there is no tradition in Hong Kong of hypothecating particular revenue to particular uses, it might have been possible to demonstrate that the yield from the charge was no greater than the expenditure incurred in manning the border crossings. The charge was also seen as a reasonable analogue to the existing airport departure tax. With some 87 million land and sea departures in 2006, such a levy could produce a significant, if not spectacular yield, perhaps comparable to the $1.5 billion accruing annually from the airport departure tax. Intuitively, if people could afford the journey they should be able to afford an additional $20 or so as a border charge. But the proposal encountered some popular opposition, albeit from a minority, and the government shied away for fear of more. It tamely dropped the proposal, reasoning that the time was not ripe. While that argument may have been valid at the time on the grounds that the economy had not yet recovered from recession, it must be time-expired by now. But the administration has remained silent.

Meanwhile, there is no sign of any move which might significantly increase the progressivity of the tax structure. The complicated and highly charged issue of whether to move towards a comprehensive income tax, which would extend to unearned income, has occasionally been mentioned, but in economic, administrative and political terms it is a minefield, and little serious effort has been made to take the debate forward.

One route to greater progressivity could lie in real estate. The administrative basis for such taxation — rates — already exists. Currently, rates yield some $15 billion a year. Avoidance is tricky: everyone needs somewhere to live and — unlike income, or financial investments, or even consumption — a house or flat is immobile and verifiable. Moreover, in very general terms the value of properties is roughly proportional to the wealth or income of the occupants; you do not find tycoons slumming it. One might therefore contemplate moving towards a progressive structure for domestic rates, rather than the flat rate, currently pitched at 5% of assessed rental value. Such a system could be designed so as not to impact adversely on the middle classes and only to hit those who are plainly able to pay more.

The government may seek to explain its apparent reluctance to target more redistribution of wealth through the fiscal system by reference to the disincentive effect which higher taxation may have on enterprise and effort, and the possible negative effect on Hong Kong's attractiveness as a business location. However, if the government was really committed to raising the living standards of the poorer tranches of society by, for example, improving the quality of social support, it could probably find ways to exact more tax from the rich without pushing marginal tax rates in key areas such as salaries and profits to materially disincentivising levels, and without increasing the total burden on individuals or businesses to levels which would seriously impact on locational choices.

For the time being the gulf between rich and poor is as wide as ever, with few concrete proposals to reduce it. The inequality is not something which appears to trouble much the conscience of the rich. Nor does it provoke organised lobbying from or on behalf of the poor on a scale that might be serious enough to embarrass the government. In such quiescent circumstances, it is understandable that the government may see no great urgency to act. It has, however, appointed a Commission on Poverty (see Chapter 7), and it remains to be seen what that might recommend.

Prior questions to be answered

The discussion of future taxation has, in recent years, been conducted very much on the assumption that there is some underlying structural problem, as described above, which will only be resolvable by some rather drastic measures. But is there really such a problem? The government has produced projections of the fiscal balance up to five years ahead, which present an extremely sanguine picture (see Table 4.7), but it has not provided a breakdown between underlying and cyclical components, nor indicated secular tendencies to which elements of its income or expenditure may be subject.

Table 4.7 Government's medium range forecast for
budget surplus and public spending ($ billion)

	2006–07	2007–08	2008–09	2009–10	2010–11	2011–12
Consolidated surplus, prior to repayments of borrowing	58.6	25.4	49.6	45.7	45.4	58.7
Consolidated surplus, after repayments of borrowing, (% of GDP in brackets)	56.1 (3.8)	24.5 (1.7)	46.9 (2.9)	42.2 (2.4)	45.4 (2.5)	58.7 (3.0)
Public expenditure, % of GDP	16.7	17.4	17.0	17.1	16.8	16.3

Source: 2007–08 Budget Speech, www.budget.gov.hk; updated from government press release, 30 April 2007, reprinted by permission of the Government of the Hong Kong Special Administrative Region.

There are reasons for believing that the need to introduce new or more severe taxes may never materialise.

First, more attention could be given to the accruals-based accounts. These tend to present a more sanguine view of the annual balance. The difference arises very largely from the inclusion of the entire earnings of the Exchange Fund in the accruals version. (The Exchange Fund is more fully discussed in Chapter 5.) Although the government has always been very sensitive to any suggestion that more of the Exchange Fund's resources should be made available to the budget, there are powerful arguments for doing so, supported by practice in other jurisdictions.

Second, pessimism over the public finances is generally associated with an assumption that revenue from land sales will be significantly less buoyant in future. This view may be coloured by the memories of a few lean years of recession, but it belies a certain confusion over land policy. Given that land is scarce and the government is in effect the monopoly supplier, there is no reason why substantial revenues should not continue, the more so if government sticks to its high land price policy. Its mindset, and indeed its accounting policy where land revenue is treated as the sale of a depleting asset, suggest that it considers this to be a finite source of revenue. But in Hong Kong the government creates land through reclamation, and obtains repeat doses of revenue when existing sites come up for redevelopment.

Thus, land could produce continuing revenue, although it may not be steady from one year to the next, and will certainly continue to be more variable than, say, salaries tax. Government makes the mistake of not wanting to rely on this revenue source because it is volatile, whereas it ought to factor in an average stream of revenue, and accept that a shortfall in one year can, if necessary, be covered by resort to borrowing, which can in turn be repaid in the next buoyant year.

The government makes a similar mistake in respect of the investment return on the fiscal reserves. Because the return may be volatile from year to year, government is reluctant to rely on it, even though it yields a very secure long-term rate of return.

The third and perhaps most important reason for querying the necessity for new taxes is that it may imply defiance of the Basic Law. As the economy grows, government revenues from existing sources are likely to grow too, and probably at a somewhat faster rate. There is also a tendency for spending to grow, perhaps even more strongly. But the Basic Law limits growth on the spending side of the equation to the growth rate of the economy as a whole. This may put a lot of pressure on infrastructural and social programmes, but by one means or another — possibly by privatising certain projects and services or by raising user fees — the Law will presumably have to be adhered to. If it is, then the need for novel or exceptional measures to increase revenue may not arise.

Assessment

Hong Kong needs a coherent long-term fiscal plan. All the strands need to be drawn together. But the arrangement of government is not conducive. The civil service does not possess the expertise on all relevant matters. Principal officials are too concerned with short-term issues to spend much time on the longer term, and anyway, at present, they direct most of their energies to holding public support for the administration by not introducing anything too contentious. The advisory network and outside consultants are used to take forward particular proposals, but seldom to indulge in strategic planning. Those bodies charged with strategic thinking, such as the Central Policy Unit and Commission on Strategic Development (of which more in Chapter 7) have scarcely made any contribution at all to matters of fiscal policy.

Thus, fiscal policy limps along from one year to the next, with the minimum of measures, at the macro level, necessary to keep the consolidated account in surplus, or at least out of persistent deficit; and a sufficient collection of micro measures to give effect to prevailing plans in such fields as infrastructure, welfare and education, and to keep particular interest groups happy. Many important fundamental questions, such as how to reduce the level of housing support and eliminate abuses there (surely the direction in which a truly 'hands-off' government would be moving), the future of land policy and hence the associated revenues, the case for greater exploitation of the resources of the Exchange Fund, or the possible longer-term fiscal inflexibility arising from the Basic Law, are seemingly left in the too-difficult box.

What does the government's approach to fiscal policy tell us about the extent of its involvement in the economy? Plainly, no government can be entirely disengaged. Judging from its overall level of taxation and spending, Hong Kong appears to justify its reputation and claim as a place of minimal official interference. But such figures do not give a completely accurate picture. The government controls land supply and influences its utilisation, not just for environmental or planning reasons but in furtherance of public housing policy, infrastructural projects and sectoral economic strategies. To that end it provides subsidies, which are not necessarily explicit ones which get recorded as government spending and for which additional revenue has to be found, but implicit ones which are manifest in concessions or waivers of land charges.

Low marginal rates of taxation ensure that the tax system does not create undue distortions to decisions of economic agents between work and leisure, spending and saving, and so on. But, relative to most other advanced economies, the effective tax on land and property which arises from the government's exploitation of its monopoly position in that market is partly responsible for Hong Kong being an extremely cramped place in which to live and work. But the overall economic impact of such a distortion is difficult to discern, since the alternative would probably involve new or increased taxation in other domains.

— 5 —

Monetary Policy

Introduction

In the realm of monetary policy, Hong Kong's currency board is perhaps just about as 'hands-off' an arrangement as an economy could possibly have. Nevertheless, there have been occasions when the system has been characterised by its critics as suppressing market-determined adjustment, or when accusations of disproportionate intervention in markets have been levelled at the authorities. This chapter first reviews Hong Kong's monetary system and then briefly discusses the circumstances which have given rise to some criticism.

Hong Kong is different

Hong Kong differs from most developed economies in that, in common with just a few other small jurisdictions (for example, Bosnia-Herzegovena, Bulgaria, Estonia and Lithuania), it operates a currency board. The Hong Kong Monetary Authority, which occupies the position of central bank, effectively abjures any influence over the money supply or interest rates, but instead aims single-mindedly to maintain a fixed exchange rate, and — an important distinction between currency boards and other regimes where the authorities may be committed to a fixed rate — accepts the consequences which that brings for interest rates, money supply, and hence for inflation and other aspects of the economy which may be considered to be influenced by monetary conditions.

In other regimes which focus on a fixed rate, but without the discipline of a currency board, the central bank (or monetary authority) has some latitude to influence domestic monetary conditions over and above any impact from official operations in the foreign exchange market to sustain the exchange rate. In the case of Hong Kong, and other strict currency boards, the monetary authority is forbidden to seek to modify the domestic monetary impact of foreign exchange transactions executed for the account of the currency board.

History

Why does Hong Kong choose to differ from the mainstream of modern economies in this way? Much of the answer is rooted in Hong Kong's history as a trading post for China and a British colony.

Hong Kong's present-day economy has its origins in the colonisation of Hong Kong by Great Britain in the mid-nineteenth century, as a key trading link to China. Before the colony's administrators had had much time to think about monetary matters, the traders found it convenient, not unnaturally, to base their business on the monetary system which operated in China. That was the silver standard. When Hong Kong introduced its own currency, it was therefore based on silver — silver coinage, and banknotes which were exchangeable for silver. Broadly speaking, this was the system which prevailed through to 1935. At that point China abandoned the silver standard. Hong Kong followed suit, and shifted to what was described at the time as a managed currency. This emerged, in practice, as a currency board based on sterling.[34]

The currency board was already established as the norm for British colonies. It had been conceived as an administratively simple and financially efficient mechanism for ensuring an adequate supply of local currency notes and coins in a colony, solidly backed against sterling at a fixed rate.

In that era, most banking transactions would anyway have been conducted in sterling, so there was seldom any very compelling need to develop financial markets in the local currency. If an increasing amount of local business and banking came to be denominated in the local currency, as it certainly did in Hong Kong over the years, there was a natural tendency for the exchange rate between the local currency and the anchor currency to hold close to the fixed rate which had been set for notes and coin. In other words, the whole economy was seen to function on that fixed rate.

Indeed, in those times there was never the slightest doubt about the colony's currency remaining at its fixed rate to sterling. Having already established its separate currency denomination, albeit with a fixed rate, the colony would be enjoying the profit from currency issuance.[35] There was no compelling need to move any further towards monetary independence.

After an interruption associated with the Japanese occupation of Hong Kong during the Second World War, the sterling-based currency board continued.

The success of a currency board arrangement, and its acceptability to local people and businesses, depend to a considerable extent on the anchor currency being reasonably stable. In this context Hong Kong was tied to the fortunes of sterling. Already in 1967, when sterling devalued, Hong Kong chose not to follow sterling down, but to re-peg at a new rate which maintained the previous cross-rate against the US dollar.

Then in June 1972, another sterling crisis led to a substantial loss of purchasing power for Hong Kong's international reserves, which were almost entirely sterling-denominated, and to a depreciation of the Hong Kong dollar against non-sterling currencies which Hong Kong's own economic performance did not warrant. Hong Kong decided to cut its link with sterling. At the same time it abandoned the currency board framework.

However, without a central bank, there was no alternative framework within which the authorities could operate an effective monetary policy. Monetary stability became dependent largely on the actions of the major banks, notably HSBC. For as long as the banks' interests and objectives were broadly coincident with those of the government, there was no great problem.

This partnership worked satisfactorily for some ten years. Then in 1983 there was a crisis of confidence in Hong Kong and its currency, sparked by the instigation of discussions between the British and Chinese governments on the future of Hong Kong beyond 1997. The Hong Kong dollar began to depreciate steeply. The banks did not feel that they could risk the funds of their depositors or shareholders by supporting it further.

Because Hong Kong still had no central bank, and therefore did not have the necessary institutional infrastructure to operate a discretionary monetary policy effectively, the only means quickly available to restore a modicum of stability was to return to the discipline of the currency board. In October 1983 a currency board 'peg' was therefore re-established, on this occasion against the US dollar rather than sterling, at the rate of

HK$7.80=US$1. That is the system which, with a number of subsequent refinements, endures up to the present day.

How the currency board functions

Box 5.1 The Hong Kong Monetary Authority

The Hong Kong Monetary Authority (HKMA) was established in 1993. For most purposes, particularly concerning its functions, the main ones of which are the conduct of monetary policy (which means, in practice, for the time being, maintenance of the fixed rate against the US dollar) and the regulation and supervision of banks, the HKMA can properly be regarded as Hong Kong's central bank. There are, however, important respects in which it differs from a typical central bank.

Most significantly, the HKMA is not a corporate entity with its own balance sheet and board of directors, which would usually accompany such status. Rather, the Monetary Authority is simply the person designated by the financial secretary under the Exchange Fund Ordinance to carry out certain duties. The ordinance allows that person to engage staff and premises to assist in the discharge of those duties. This gives rise to the institution which is commonly known as the HKMA, while the designated person is known as the chief executive of the HKMA.

This means that the HKMA is directly under the authority of the financial secretary. This structure sets it apart from most of the world's central banks which nowadays enjoy a measure of statutory independence from ministers — in the sense that any ministerial intervention would usually be subject to approval or scrutiny by democratically mandated bodies.

However, Hong Kong has done its best to make good this shortcoming through an exchange of letters between the financial secretary and the Monetary Authority, which clearly specifies the division of responsibilities.* Of course, this could be overridden at any time, but such action would be highly visible and would, if the judgement on which it was based was at all contentious, risk the financial secretary attracting considerable public opprobrium.

Generally speaking, the HKMA intervenes no more in the operation of the financial sector than the overriding aims of monetary stability and banking soundness demand. In recent years it has become more proactive in promoting Hong Kong's financial services — especially in renminbi banking and in securing other Mainland business — but this has been a strategy of removing barriers and not one which, beyond that, involves interference in the workings of the market economy or any significant call on public resources.

★ (Letter from the financial secretary to the Monetary Authority, 25 June 2003, available at www.hkma.gov.hk, reprinted by permission of the Government of the Hong Kong Special Administrative Region.)

The system has evolved since 1983 as a result of a number of adjustments and refinements, but always with the overriding objective of keeping the exchange rate against the US dollar at close to 7.80. As the system stands today, it operates according to the rules and principles summarised in Box 5.2.

Box 5.2   Hong Kong's currency board: Rules and mechanism

Basic rules

'Stock' rule: the monetary base (which comprises certificates of indebtedness, compulsorily held by note-issuing banks as exact backing for their note issue; the settlement balances of banks held at the Exchange Fund; and Exchange Fund bills and notes in issue (which banks can readily convert into settlement balances), must at all times be fully backed by US dollars at the rate of 7.80.

'Flow' rule: any increases/decreases in the aggregate monetary base must be matched by equivalent transactions against US dollars with the Exchange Fund, at intervention rates in the range 7.75–7.85 in the case of banks' balances, or 7.80 in the case of certificates of indebtedness.

Operational mechanism

Certificates of indebtedness are bought from the Exchange Fund against payment in US dollars at the rate of 7.80 when the note issue expands, and redeemed for value in US dollars at the rate of 7.80 when the note issue contracts.

At any time a bank may have Hong Kong dollars credited to its settlement account at the Exchange Fund by selling US dollars to the Fund at the rate of 7.75. At any time a bank may acquire US dollars from the Fund by selling Hong Kong dollars to it at the rate of 7.85, but only to the extent that it has the necessary Hong Kong dollar funds in its settlement account, or can obtain such funds through sale and repurchase transactions in Exchange Fund bills or notes with the Fund.

The HKMA may at its discretion execute HK/US dollar-exchange transactions with banks, for HK dollar settlement across the banks' settlement accounts, at rates inside the range 7.75–7.85.

A bank may carry out sale and repurchase transactions with the Exchange Fund during the course of the business day to cover shortfalls in its clearing balance arising from the interbank settlement process. No interest is charged. If the debit balance is not cleared by the end of the day, the bank must cover it by, effectively, borrowing from the Fund — through overnight repos in EFBN. Such borrowings will be subject to an interest charge according to the discount rate formula, which embodies a penalty element.

Box 5.3 illustrates the expected adjustment processes in response to upward and downward pressure on the exchange rate. (Note that a higher number for the exchange rate expressed as Hong Kong dollars per US dollar — e.g. 7.90 rather than 7.80 — implies a weaker Hong Kong dollar exchange rate.) From the point of view of the debate about government intervention in the economy, the key aspect of the arrangements is that they involve a minimum of discretion by officials.

Box 5.3   Hong Kong's currency board: Adjustment

Response Mechanism to Strong Hong Kong Dollar

Excess of market participants wishing to buy Hong Kong dollars
Upward pressure on Hong Kong dollar
Market exchange rate strengthens towards 7.75
When the rate hits 7.75, HKMA buys US dollars at 7.75, crediting
    Hong Kong dollar proceeds to banks' settlement accounts
Monetary base expands
Resultant extra liquidity puts downward pressure on interest rates
Lower interest rates and abundant liquidity serve as disincentive to
    holding or acquiring Hong Kong dollars
Upward pressure on exchange rate therefore abates
Exchange rate weakens away from the 7.75 limit — back towards
    7.80.

Other possible longer-term elements in the monetary adjustment
mechanism

Additional liquidity and cheaper credit, if they persisted, would
stimulate consumption and investment spending, and prompt
inflationary pressure. Any extra spending would feed through to
additional demand for imports, while any additional inflation would
impair competitiveness. Both these developments would tend to
weaken the exchange rate and so assist the equilibrating process.

Response Mechanism to Weak Hong Kong Dollar

Excess of market participants wishing to sell Hong Kong dollars
Downward pressure on Hong Kong dollar
Market exchange rate weakens towards 7.85
When the rate hits 7.85, HKMA sells US dollars at 7.85, debiting
    Hong Kong dollars from banks' settlement accounts
Monetary base contracts
Tighter liquidity puts upward pressure on interest rates
Higher interest rates and shortage of liquidity serve as incentive to
    holding or acquiring Hong Kong dollars
Downward pressure on exchange rate therefore abates

Exchange rate strengthens away from 7.85 limit — back towards 7.80.

Other possible longer-term elements in the monetary adjustment mechanism

Tighter liquidity and dearer credit, if they persisted, would dampen consumption and investment spending, and reduce or reverse inflationary pressure. Any reduction in spending would feed through to weaker demand for imports, while any reduction in inflation would benefit competitiveness. Both these developments would tend to strengthen the exchange rate and so assist the equilibrating process.

Hong Kong would be perfectly capable of operating an alternative monetary regime, such as the inflation targeting which is widely practised among other developed economies. But inflation targeting is less precise in a small, highly open economy than it is in a larger, more closed one, and nobody has demonstrated in a convincing manner that Hong Kong's underlying economic performance would thereby be enhanced. Moreover, any regime which appeared to carry less specific policy prescriptions and to involve greater judgmental discretion by the Monetary Authority or financial secretary would be more open to political pressures. There does not appear, therefore, to be any compelling reason for change.

The Exchange Fund

The Exchange Fund is integral to the exchange rate regime, since, among other things, it holds the foreign currency backing required by the currency board system. The Fund is an account of the Hong Kong government. However, it is unique across the government's financial activities in that it lies outside the ambit of the usual budgetary process. Whereas budgetary expenditure is subject to approval by the Legislative Council, the Exchange Fund is under the direct control of the financial secretary — albeit advised by an Exchange Fund Advisory Committee.

The investment of the Fund's assets is performed by the Monetary Authority, which also prepares and publishes the accounts. The assets do not, however, belong to the Monetary Authority, although the costs of running the Authority are, once approved by the financial secretary, met from the Exchange Fund.

Table 5.1   The Exchange Fund: Balance sheet at the end of 2006

Assets	HK$ billion
cash and placements with banks and other financial institutions	64
securities	1,089
other	23
Total	1,176
of which	
Hong Kong dollar assets	*131*
Foreign currency assets	*1,045*
Liabilities	
certificates of indebtedness	156
government-issued notes and coin	7
balance of banking system	2
Exchange Fund bills and notes	129
placements by banks and other financial institutions	8
fiscal reserve	325
other	41
total liabilities	668
accumulated surplus	508
total liabilities and equity	1,176

Note: Placements with or by banks represent essentially the management of working balances and the activities of the HKMA in the interbank market, where the HKMA may borrow funds (which appear as a liability) or place funds (as an asset).

Source: HKMA *Annual Report*.

A simplified balance sheet of the Exchange Fund, as at the end of 2006, is shown in Table 5.1.

For analytical purposes the liabilities side of the balance sheet may conveniently be regarded as comprising the following four main items:

(a) the currency component, consisting of the certificates of indebtedness which serve as backing for the banknotes issued by the note-issuing banks, together with a relatively small amount of currency (ten-dollar notes and all coinage) issued by the government; the currency component totals $163 billion in the table;

(b) the banking and money market component, comprising Exchange Fund bills and notes in issue, banks' balances (the sum of all the balances which individual banks hold with the Fund for interbank settlement purposes), and any other placements by banks or other financial institutions; this component totals $139 billion;

(c) the government component, comprising the fiscal reserve: the government passes its budget surpluses to the Fund for safekeeping and investment; the outstanding accumulated amount totals $325 billion;

(d) the accumulated surplus of the Fund itself, which is the profits retained from its investments over the years; the proportion of profits apportionable to the fiscal reserve is paid to the government; the remainder is retained in the Fund; although there is a statutory provision in the Exchange Fund Ordinance for larger sums to be transferred back to the budget, this has never been exercised; the surplus totals $508 billion.

As regards the assets, the foreign currency component equates to Hong Kong's foreign currency reserves or, in alternative terminology, its international reserves. Most of the Hong Kong dollar element is accounted for by equity investments which were originally acquired as a result of the 1998 stock market intervention (see below). After that episode the decision was taken to retain a portfolio of Hong Kong equities equivalent to a target 5% of the Exchange Fund's assets,[36] while selling off the remainder of the shares acquired during the intervention through the Tracker Fund, which was launched in 2000.[37]

Hong Kong's foreign reserves are amongst the highest in the world. The rules of the currency board require that the monetary liabilities of the Fund — essentially items (a) and (b) above — must be fully backed by US dollar assets. This is plainly fulfilled by a huge margin (almost 80% of the foreign currency assets are held in US dollars). Beyond that monetary requirement, the government has never presented any rigorous assessment as to what level of reserves should desirably be held. Generally speaking, however, a conservative and ostensibly mercantilist attitude prevails — holding a 'war chest' against unforeseen events and deriving some satisfaction from a high ranking in international league tables of official reserves.[38]

Conservative caution is even used as a basis for arguing that the fiscal reserve, which is invested through the Exchange Fund in foreign assets which form part of the international reserves, must be kept intact in order to safeguard those foreign reserves. As foreshadowed in the preceding chapter, however, that argument is largely spurious. It confuses assets and liabilities.

If the government draws down its fiscal reserve, the Monetary Authority must decide how to fund the drawdown. It can of course sell foreign currency assets, but it is wrong to assume that it must do so. The most obvious alternative would be for the Fund to borrow Hong Kong dollars, either from the interbank market or by issuing additional securities. The investments of the Fund would not need to be touched. It is certainly common practice in other economies for target levels of international reserves to be sustained, when necessary, by satisfying government financing needs from official borrowing, rather than by drawing down international reserves. There is no reason why Hong Kong should not consider doing likewise in the event of budget deficits.

The conservative stance also explains why, despite occasional pressure from other quarters, successive financial secretaries have never displayed the slightest inclination to seek to 'raid' the Exchange Fund, by invoking the statutory procedure (enshrined in the Exchange Fund Ordinance) to transfer surplus funds from the Fund to the general budget. As noted above, the surplus amounted to $508 billion at the end of 2006. In most other jurisdictions this would be incorporated automatically into the mainstream government accounts, and it is indeed treated thus in Hong Kong's accrual-based accounts. But, despite occasional pressure from some legislative councillors and other quarters, especially in recessionary times, to make funds available from this source for budgetary expenditure, official prudence and caution have always prevailed.

Manipulating competitiveness?

Despite the currency board's tightly rules–based approach, which leaves little of any significance to the discretion of the authorities, it has at times been suggested that the fixed exchange rate can itself be a mechanism for unfairly manipulating the economy's competitiveness. This would refer to occasions when the currency appears to be undervalued and is therefore subject to upward pressure. By resisting such pressure, Hong Kong might be placed in the same camp as China, which has been criticised in recent years by the United States and others for managing its rate so as to limit appreciation against the US dollar.

There are, however, fundamental differences between the currency regimes of the Mainland and Hong Kong. Hong Kong allows free movements of capital into and out of the territory, and allows these to impact automatically on domestic monetary conditions, thus sparking the type of adjustments described in Box 5.3. Any attempt to offset these consequences through financial operations by the Monetary Authority (so-called open-market operations) is prohibited. So the entire process is very much hands-off.

China, by contrast, continues to exercise control over capital movements, despite some progressive liberalisation in recent years. And the Chinese authorities obstruct market-driven adjustments to inflows (or outflows) by exercising their discretion to intervene in both the foreign exchange market and the domestic financial markets. The upshot of all this is that, whereas in Hong Kong any perceived undervaluation of the exchange rate will result in capital inflows, increased liquidity and eventually faster inflation which will eliminate the original undervaluation, in China attempts are made to suppress some or all of those consequences, with the further result that the perceived undervaluation persists.

Box 5.4   A digression: The Hong Kong dollar and the renminbi

It is worth noting — because it is a topical issue rather than because it has any direct relevance to the focus of this book — that pegging the Hong Kong dollar to the renminbi would not be a particularly sensible move in present circumstances. Under existing Mainland rules the Hong Kong Exchange Fund would not be permitted to invest in renminbi assets, so it would not be possible to operate a proper currency board based on the mainland currency. Fixing to the renminbi would therefore require a more active intervention strategy. More generally, it would be unwise for a fully convertible currency to declare a fixed rate against a non-convertible one, not least because it is unclear how that currency would behave once it became more convertible, especially with a central bank inexperienced in managing a convertible currency.

Anyway, in terms of macroeconomic adjustment between the two economies, because of their divergent stages of development one must expect continuing shifts over time in the real exchange rate between the Mainland and Hong Kong. Although it is perfectly feasible to achieve such adjustment through differential rates of domestic inflation, the ability of the nominal exchange rate to alter would be an added dimension for adjustment. In that sense, the maintenance by Hong Kong of a fixed rate to the US dollar while retaining the ability to shift with the US dollar against the renminbi might be preferable to maintaining a fixed link to the latter. In other words, there would be no advantage to Hong Kong in shifting its peg from the US to the Chinese currency.

In the longer term, when the Mainland has established a track record in managing a fully convertible currency, and when the structural and developmental gap between Hong Kong and the Mainland has narrowed, it might well make sense to peg or even unify the two currencies. But the fact that Hong Kong is already highly dependent on the Mainland economy, is not a sufficient reason for making such a move in the near term.

Events of August 1998

Another, more voluble accusation of interventionism arose in relation to the events of August 1998 when the Monetary Authority intervened heavily in the foreign exchange and stock markets.

Briefly, following on from the Asian financial turmoil of 1997 and the associated depreciations of several other regional currencies relative to the US dollar, the Hong Kong dollar began to come under pressure. The HKMA intervened heavily in the markets to thwart market manipulation by certain dominant market players. This was not an attempt to stop normal speculation of a price-taking nature. The action was justified because the free play of market forces, on which speculators normally thrive, was being swamped by actions to manipulate prices in an anti-competitive manner.[39]

Box 5.5 The Hong Kong crisis, 1998

Following on from the Asian financial turmoil, the Hong Kong dollar came under pressure. There was evidence of significant market manipulation by one or two large players, big enough to move the Hong Kong market (i.e. price-setters rather than just price-takers).

Examples are as follows (all figures are illustrative only).

Manipulator's strategy

Manipulator sells futures contracts in the Hang Sang stock market index at a price of, say, 10,000 (quite close to prevailing spot level); the contracts will mature in two weeks' time.

The manipulator then sells Hong Kong dollars in the foreign exchange market; at that time the HKMA was a willing buyer at about 7.75 (and would certainly have been willing to defend the rate exhaustively at 7.80). Note that the manipulator may have borrowed the Hong Kong dollars earlier at relatively low interest rates.

The manipulator would presume that this intervention would be for the currency board account, in which case it would cause a drain of liquidity from the money market and so drive up interest rates according to the classical currency board mechanism; this is the key manipulative move — the ability of one big player to significantly influence interest rates in the relatively small Hong Kong money market.

The manipulator would predict that the squeeze on liquidity and higher interest rates would cause share prices, and hence the Hang Seng index, to fall — say to 9,000.

The manipulator would then hope to purchase futures contracts at around 9,000 in order to close out his position.

He would also expect to be able, if he wished, to square his short Hong Kong dollar position in the foreign exchange market, by buying back Hong Kong dollars, at a rate not significantly different from the 7.75 at which he sold them (since the HKMA would not be prepared to see the rate strengthen much beyond that for fear of undermining the credibility of the currency board system).

This sequence of transactions would, if followed through in the manner described, result in a short-term profit in the region of 10% for the manipulator.

HKMA's response

In order to thwart the above process the HKMA decided to meet a substantial part of the selling pressure against the Hong Kong dollar by supplying US dollars from outside the currency board account, in a manner which would not result in upward pressure on interest rates. This was an entirely legitimate tactic, despite the currency board regime, since it did not affect the monetary base and because it left intact the full foreign currency cover for the monetary base.

The HKMA also made massive purchases of shares in the stock market — amounting to almost 10% of the Hang Seng index. This action succeeded in holding up share prices and imposing large losses on the manipulators when they had to close out their short positions.

These actions together ensured that the Hong Kong dollar remained stable, the rise in interest rates was short-lived, and the government's Exchange Fund made huge profits when share prices subsequently recovered further and most of the shareholdings were sold back to investors.

This action did not infringe any currency board rules, since most of the HKMA's interventions were conducted outside the currency board system. But it did represent clear activism by the authorities. This was justifiable as necessary to preserve and protect the proper operation of markets, in the face of anti-competitive behaviour by a few. The essence of efficient and fair markets is that each player should be a price-taker, able to choose to buy or sell goods — or financial instruments — at the prevailing price, but not able to dictate that price or manipulate it to his advantage. If a player is so dominant as to be able to dictate the price — or at least to move it by a significant amount — the market ceases to be a free competitive market and official intervention to correct the anomaly is justified. This, in essence, is what happened in August 1998. It fell within the government's rightful mandate to ensure a fair and competitive business climate.

Day-to-day intervention in operating the currency board

In terms of delivering exchange rate stability against the US dollar, Hong Kong's currency board since 1983 has been remarkably successful. Even so, the history of the period shows that, far from being a shining example of the textbook currency board delivering a fixed rate through an automatic adjustment mechanism, the day-to-day management of Hong Kong's currency board system has embodied a considerable amount of discretionary intervention by the authorities in the foreign exchange and money markets.[40]

An analysis of the performance of the currency board suggests that such discretionary intervention was necessary in the early years after 1983 in order to keep the exchange rate stable, but that from 1988 to 1998 the authorities may have prolonged such practices unnecessarily. They seemed reluctant to desist from seeking to influence interbank liquidity and interest rates, although some of that reluctance may have been justified in order to prevent undue domination of the market by the single largest bank. Since 1998 the intervention has been progressively reduced, and only a small residual amount remains exercisable today — namely the scope for the HKMA to intervene in the foreign exchange market inside the band delineated by its formal undertakings to sell US dollars to banks at 7.85 or buy from them at 7.75. It is far from clear why the HKMA needs to retain that intra-limits discretion, although it is difficult to argue that it is harmful.

In sum, the success of the 7.80 peg in the early years certainly owed much to the exercise of discretionary intervention. As the years passed, although retention of discretion was not obviously damaging, the authorities may have clung on to it rather longer than they needed to. In terms of the broader question about government intervention in the workings of the economy, these departures from strict hands-off principles are scarcely of great significance.

Conclusion

This chapter has reviewed the operation of monetary policy in the particular context of identifying instances where official tactics might be considered at odds with Hong Kong's 'hands-off' image. Broadly speaking, the authorities emerge with a pretty clean bill of health. Allegations of manipulating competitiveness or of compromising free-market principles during the 1998 crisis are found to lack substance. Discretionary intervention in the day-to-day running of the currency board, though needed in the early stages to ensure that the system succeeded, may have been prolonged unnecessarily, but is not nowadays significant. Meanwhile, it could be argued that, by never drawing on the Exchange Fund's surpluses for budgetary purposes, the government may actually have been overzealous in its 'hands-off' self-denial.

– 6 –

Competition Policy and Competitiveness

Government stance on competition policy

Even the most ardent advocates of *laissez-faire* would accept that appropriate laws and regulations need to be in force governing various aspects of business or personal life. Most countries recognise, in this context, the need to control or eliminate monopolies and cartels that may operate against the public interest. In Hong Kong, the government's philosophy of non-interference, coupled to its often close ties with leading business personalities, has made it reluctant to introduce wide-ranging pro-competition legislation, although it has constantly avowed itself to be firmly in favour of fair competition and — as evidenced, for example, by its action in 1998 in the stock market, described in the preceding chapter — opposed to any forms of market manipulation.

The government's overall approach to the issue of competition has come under increasing challenge. In May 1998 the government, through the Competition Policy Advisory Group (COMPAG), which is a forum under the financial secretary's chairmanship with the remit to review policy issues related to competition, issued a statement of its stance on competition policy.[41] It declared that it was committed to competition, not as an end in itself but as a means to "enhance economic efficiency and free flow of trade, thereby also benefiting consumer welfare", and that it considered competition to best be nurtured and sustained by allowing the free play of market forces and keeping intervention to the minimum. Thus,

> We will not interfere with market forces simply on the basis of the number
> of operators, scale of operations, or normal commercial constraints faced by

new entrants. We will take action only when market imperfections or distortions limit market accessibility or market contestability, and impair economic efficiency or free trade, to the detriment of the overall interest of Hong Kong . . . . The determination of whether a practice is restrictive, detrimental to economic efficiency or free trade, and against the overall interest of Hong Kong must be made in the light of the actual situation. The intended purpose and effects of the practice in question, and the relevant market or economic conditions, etc., must all be taken into account.

The statement also listed various examples of restrictive practices which should be "attended" to; these included: price-fixing, bid-rigging, market allocation, sales and production quotas, joint boycotts, and unfair or discriminatory standards. It also included an illustrative list of abuses of market position, e.g. predatory behaviour such as selling below cost; setting retail price minimums for products or services where there are no ready substitutes; and conditioning the supply of specific products or services to the purchase of other specific products or services.

The government was of the opinion, at that time, that there was

no international standard or consensus on what is the best approach to achieve competition. . . . For Hong Kong, a small and externally-oriented economy which is already highly competitive, the Government sees no need to enact an all-embracing competition law.

The government said that it would nevertheless be active in promoting competition and watchful for obstacles and instances of uncompetitive behaviour. It favoured a sectoral approach to tackling any problems. Attention was drawn to the Consumer Council's work in drawing up codes of practice that promote competition. Also, under the auspices of COMPAG, the authorities have adopted a number of initiatives to enhance competition, and have taken follow-up actions on many competition-related complaints.[42]

Pressure for change

There have been longstanding critics of the government's reluctance to take more forthright action to promote competition. A flavour of such criticism can be found in the accompanying extracts from a speech given by one respected commentator in 2002 (see Box 6.1). Much of what is said there still holds true today.

Box 6.1   A view of competition versus collusion, from 2002

(Extracts from a speech by Philip Bowring to the Hong Kong Democratic Foundation in July 2002; www.hkdf.org. Reprinted by permission of Mr Philip Bowring.)

Conspiracy to raise prices against the public interest is a natural objective of businessmen. Price competition is uncomfortable. The closer the government — which exists to maintain law and a level playing field — comes to such businessmen, the greater the danger that their sectional interests will dominate, at public expense.

[Consider] the supermarket duopoly — two firms which have proved incapable of competing overseas. One of the most efficient global firms, Carrefour, was forced to withdraw [plans to set up in Hong Kong] because of what amounted to a conspiracy by local interests to deprive it of prime sites and by suppliers with monopolies protected by laws against parallel imports. In many countries the behaviour of some of Hong Kong's leading businesses would be criminal offences.

Much of the domestic economy is in the hands of oligopolies, formal or informal. There is the power duopoly resulting in excess capacity, zero price competition, high prices and assured return on capital. There is the port situation, whereby existing operators campaign against local expansion but expand on the mainland, thus protecting high margins here while finding growth elsewhere.

Then there is Cathay Pacific whose interests are limiting Hong Kong's hub role.

The depredations of the property cartel are notorious. Note the cartel-like behaviour of the big developers and the unnatural linkages between them and the banks. The difference between mortgages available on new as compared with, say, 15-year-old flats is a disgraceful mutual back-scratching exercise which has nothing to do with sound banking and a lot to do with corporate cronyism. The proximity of government figures to one or two developers in particular has meant that being friendly to this business has taken precedence over most others as the twists and turns in public housing, land sales and tax policy indicate. Cyberport was a particularly egregious example of cronyism which has done Hong Kong immense damage. But there have been plenty of others.

The linkages between established businesses, anxious to protect their positions, and the government are much greater than is usually acknowledged — and have been getting closer. Middle to upper-level bureaucrats have moved into the private sector, whether before or after retirement. In theory such cross-fertilisation might sound beneficial to both. In practice, how much of it has been payment for services previously rendered? To land or buildings officials for generous interpretations of plot ratios or development guidelines? To policemen or fire officers for providing special services. This is an old problem but badly needs to be addressed.

More recently a different link between government and private sector has been established: management of quasi-public enterprises. Most notorious was the shift of a senior bureaucrat to an even bigger salary as chief executive of Hong Kong Exchanges and Clearing. This company is itself a monopoly which has done scant good to Hong Kong's financial services sector by maintaining minimum commissions and making a miserable job of policing listed companies and new listings. Of course, the policing job ought to be in the hands of the Securities and Futures Commission, but it doesn't seem too keen to take on a job which, if done well, would make it unpopular with the business figures who have grown richer than ever by abusing minority shareholders' rights. The SFC itself is in the hands of a bureaucrat who apparently did not see anything inappropriate in contributing to Tung Chee Hwa's re-election campaign. So much for politically independent civil servants.

Likewise we find other quango jobs taken up by members of the business elite. These are testimony to the ever closer links between government and established, locally oriented big business. Now, with the so-called responsibility system, with ministers and a few Legislative Council members sitting on the Executive Council, we have yet another shift of power towards the interests of established business groups. . . . This is all the more alarming when the government seems to want to do more, not less, to use public money to spur new industries.

For its part, the Consumer Council has felt that not enough can be achieved through mere codes of good practice. As long ago as 1996, it recommended the enactment of a competition law, to cover horizontal and vertical collusive agreements and abuse of a dominant position.[43] Meanwhile, over the years, critics of the official stance have noted that there appears to be a lack of consistency and clarity in policy, with, for example, the telecommunications sector being subjected to strong pro-competition regulation while electricity supply remains in the hands of two monopolies – one for Hong Kong Island and the other for the remainder of the territory. The evident benefits of plummeting telecom tariffs, in marked contrast to electricity charges, is seen as proof enough of the economic case for a more forthright policy approach.

It has also been noted that China is in the process of introducing anti-monopoly laws, and that Singapore passed a comprehensive competition law in 2004, so that Hong Kong is left as perhaps the only significant economy without such a law.[44] COMPAG is regarded as weak; it is anyway only advisory; and the Consumer Council is seen as having insufficient powers of investigation.

Under evident pressure from the tide of opinion, not least from WTO and IMF (see Chapter 2), the financial secretary in his 2005 budget announced the establishment of a Competition Policy Review Committee, and the chief executive took up the issue in his policy address of October 2005. Thus:

> as Hong Kong enterprises grow in strength, with some acquiring world-class status, coupled with an increased presence of multinational enterprises, it is possible that forces capable of cornering the market may emerge in Hong Kong . . . The newly established independent Committee, chaired by a Non-official with members drawn from different sectors, is tasked to review the effectiveness of our existing competition policy. The Committee will consider, among other things, whether the implementation of our policy is in line with the times, and whether available investigative powers are adequate. The Committee will also draw on international experience and discuss the need to introduce in Hong Kong a comprehensive and cross-sector law on fair competition, as well as its scope and application. The Committee expects its review to be completed in mid-2006. . . . We do not seek to intervene in the market. Rather, we want to actively protect market order and fair competition by preventing manipulative practices such as price fixing, bid rigging and market sharing. Any additional measures, including legislation, will aim to facilitate new ventures by

individuals and help small and medium enterprises operate and grow. We can take reference from the comprehensive competition laws enacted in scores of jurisdictions so that we can avoid as far as possible any negative impact stemming from legislation or other related measures. Hong Kong enterprises have always embraced competition and thrived in a competitive setting. I believe they will support our effort in maintaining a climate of free and fair competition.

The review committee submitted its report to government in June 2006. The key thrust of the report was to recommend that a competition law be drawn up (see Box 6.2). In November 2006 the government launched a public discussion document,[45] building on the report but scrupulously maintaining an open mind. The responses deadline was set at early February 2007.

Box 6.2   Key recommendations from the "Report on the review of Hong Kong's competition policy", the Competition Policy Review Committee, June 2006★

1. New legislation should be introduced to guard against anti-competitive conduct that would have an adverse effect on economic efficiency and free trade in Hong Kong.
2. Rather than target individual sectors of the economy, the legislation should apply to all.
3. Provision should be included . . . to allow the Government to grant exemptions . . . in defined circumstances on public policy or economic grounds.
4. The regulatory authority should have the discretion to disregard inappropriate complaints, so as to guard against the new law being used to stifle legitimate competitive business activities.
5. The new law would *not* target market structures, nor seek to regulate 'natural' monopolies or mergers and acquisitions.
6. The new legislation should cover the following types of anti-competitive conduct: price-fixing; bid-rigging; market allocation; sales and production quotas; joint boycotts; unfair or discriminatory standards; abuse of a dominant market position.
7. Such conduct should not be an offence *per se,* but rather, the particular conduct must be proven — (a) to have been carried out with the intent to distort the market; or (b) to have the effect of distorting normal market operation.

8. There should not be lengthy and detailed descriptions of these types of conduct in the law as such. Appropriate guidelines should be drawn up by the regulatory authority in consultation with relevant stakeholders that would include: detailed descriptions and examples of the types of anti-competitive conduct listed in the law; an indication as to how intent and effect in relation to market distortion might be assessed; and reference to cases dealt with under existing local sector-specific laws and related overseas legislation.

9. A regulatory authority, to be known as the Competition Commission should be established under the new law. The Commission should have a 'two-tier' structure, comprising a governing board underpinned by an executive arm that would include staff with relevant expertise.

10. The Commission should have an advocacy role, and should be tasked with keeping the scope and application of the new law under review.

11. The Commission should have sufficient powers to allow it to investigate thoroughly any suspected anti-competitive conduct prohibited by the new legislation.

12. The Government should seriously consider the merits of establishing a Competition Tribunal to hear cases brought by the Commission and to hand down sanctions.

13. With regard to sanctions, civil penalties should apply in cases where anti-competitive conduct is found to have occurred.

14. The Commission should be able to apply for an order from the Competition Tribunal (if established) to require an offender to cease and desist from anti-competitive conduct, pending a decision on the case.

★ Full report available at www.cedb.gov.hk, reprinted by permission of the Government of the Hong Kong Special Administrative Region.

It can be seen that, over the years, the government's position has shifted from forthright opposition to general pro-competition legislation, to what seems to be a clear willingness to go down that road if the consensus of public opinion favours it.

Competitiveness

The rationale for any measures aimed at ensuring competition is that this provides the basis for greater economic efficiency, in the sense of a better allocation of resources and enhanced output per unit of input and hence, *inter alia*, stronger international competitiveness.

The ultimate success or failure of an economy hinges on productivity and competitiveness, but competitiveness is an elusive concept. Apart from being aided by a properly competitive business climate, it also depends on there being a stable monetary environment. But, contrary to some beliefs, monetary policy itself cannot manipulate long-term competitiveness in a free market economy: currency depreciation can only assist competitiveness in the short-term, before inflationary consequences are felt. Similarly, whether the budget is in surplus or deficit, today or tomorrow, is not going to determine competitiveness. However, competitiveness will be affected by the nature of the fiscal regime — the extent to which it is friendly to business, entrepreneurship and work-effort, for example, and the extent to which a large public sector may crowd out a more efficient private sector.

Underlying competitiveness is mostly all about getting the supply side of the economy right. The Hong Kong government talks a lot about being business-friendly — keeping taxes low, minimising red tape, etc. — and developing human capital through better education. Some would argue that this is indeed as far as government needs to go, and that other policies directed at supporting or encouraging particular sectors are either unnecessary or positively damaging.

The indicators referenced in Table 2.1 show that there is quite a wide spectrum of perceptions as to the attraction of Hong Kong and its competitiveness. But, ultimately, competitiveness is manifest from results, not perceptions. A high standard of living and high value added per unit of input provide proof. It is a mistake to look simply at crude price comparisons. On that sort of logic, London would have long ago ceased to be the financial heart of Europe, Manhattan would have been eclipsed by New Jersey, Switzerland would be bankrupt, and Vientiane would be the hub of southeast Asia. It is comparative advantage which determines the allocation of different activities between different locations. It is absolute advantage (e.g. in terms of quality of capital, labour and technology) which determines overall prosperity.

These considerations are especially pertinent when looking at the relative merits of Hong Kong on the one hand, and Shenzhen or Shanghai on the other. It is not a question of whether Hong Kong will survive, but at what level it will survive. If it possesses strong intrinsic attributes, such as of skilled human capital, efficient markets and efficiency at the workplace, it will prosper as a high value-added economy. If it lacks those and reverts to an unskilled, cheap labour environment, it will fare less well. That would not necessarily mean absolute decline, but rather a situation in which it was slipping down the league table of living standards.

Box 6.3   Examples of supply-side considerations relevant to Hong Kong

Business-friendly
Minimise red-tape; keep taxes low; facilitate dissemination of business information and promotional material via Trade Development Council, Invest Hong Kong, etc.

Level playing field
Ensure free and fair competition within Hong Kong, and in market access for Hong Kong business elsewhere, e.g. the Mainland, under the auspices of CEPA.

Location-friendly
Ensure that Hong Kong is attractive as a physical location. This includes quality of life, especially from the perspective of foreigners coming to reside or Hong Kongers who might be tempted to leave; availability of accommodation or school places; the ability of spouses or other family members to integrate socially, to be permitted to work if they so wish, and to find such work; the physical environment, including pollution; and so on.

Critical mass
Survival as a business hub depends on agglomeration of activities; this will tend to happen naturally if other factors (such as business friendliness) are conducive; it may be a difficult judgement as to whether to artificially support some individual activities in order to sustain critical mass.

Human resource quality
This is extremely important. The key role of education in providing

workers with the right skills. The crucial importance of language proficiency: Putonghua is exerting a strong pull, but there appears to be a damaging ambivalence towards English.

Conclusion

It is in these areas on the supply side of the economy that a government most obviously has a role to play, even in the predominantly *laissez-faire* climate of an espoused market economy — indeed, the more so if the market economy is to function optimally. Successive Hong Kong governments have been quite diligent in attending to such issues, but it is not clear whether they have always recognised the boundary between facilitating economic activity and directing it.

PART III

The Policy Process

– 7 –

The Institutional Framework

Introduction

Hong Kong practises executive-led government. Policies are handed down by the chief executive of the Hong Kong SAR (prior to July 1997 the British-appointed governor) on the advice of the Executive Council. The Legislative Council has a role in passing laws and approving budgetary disbursements, but only in strictly limited circumstances can it formally originate policy.

In order to understand the way in which policy — in the context of this book, economic policy in particular — evolves, one must appreciate not only the constitutional structure of the chief executive and the Executive and Legislative Councils, but also the role of many advisory and consultative procedures in which the government engages, and the contribution of political parties, other pressure groups and think-tanks. This chapter describes this institutional framework in broad terms.

Chief executive

According to the Basic Law[46] the chief executive of the Hong Kong Special Administrative Region "shall be selected by election or through consultations held locally and be appointed by the Central People's Government". In practice, there is an electoral college in Hong Kong (known as the Election Committee), members of which are appointed from four broad categories and the majority of whom, thus far at least, can be presumed to be compliant with Beijing's wishes.

Tellingly, the Basic Law includes the provisions that:

> The method for selecting the Chief Executive shall be specified in the light of the actual situation in the Hong Kong Special Administrative Region and in accordance with the principle of gradual and orderly progress. The ultimate aim is the selection of the Chief Executive by universal suffrage upon nomination by a broadly representative nominating committee in accordance with democratic procedures.

and, further, that

> If there is a need to amend the method for selecting the Chief Executives for the terms subsequent to the year 2007, such amendments must be made with the endorsement of a two-thirds majority of all the members of the Legislative Council and the consent of the Chief Executive, and they shall be reported to the Standing Committee of the National People's Congress for approval.

For the moment, progress towards universal suffrage in electing the chief executive, or the entirety of the Legislative Council, is extremely slow.

Principal officials

The chief executive is supported by a 'cabinet' of 14 principal officials, appointed under the so-called Accountability System, introduced in 2002. As explained officially:

> Principal officials under the accountability system are the most important officials within the Government. They will be accountable to the Chief Executive for the success or failure of matters falling within their respective portfolios. They will accept total responsibility and, in an extreme case, they may have to step down for serious failures relating to their respective portfolios. These include serious failures in policy outcome and serious mishaps in the implementation of the relevant policies. They may also have to step down for grave personal misconduct or if they cease to be eligible under the Basic Law.
>
> They will be appointed to the Executive Council and will be responsible for all aspects of their portfolios: from determining policy objectives and goals, to policy initiation, policy formulation, policy implementation and policy outcome.[47]

In the eyes of many critics this was a flawed initiative. It saw the chief executive appointing his preferred candidates, whether from within or outside the civil service, to become principal officials and thus reinforcing a style of government that was already seen as too autocratic.

Permanent secretaries and the civil service

The government structure beneath the principal officials is basically the traditional civil service. But the most senior person in each policy bureau, designated a permanent secretary, actually has a role in providing political support to the principal officials. His or her role is

(a) to assist the principal officials in formulating, explaining and defending policies, securing support of the public and LegCo and answering LegCo questions, moving bills and taking part in motion debates in plenary sessions of LegCo. Subject to the direction of the relevant principal officials, permanent secretaries and other civil servants will explain and defend policies in public including at meetings of LegCo panels and committees;

(b) to steer and coordinate with the executive departments falling within the respective portfolios of the principal officials and liaise with other concerned bureaux to achieve smooth, timely and effective implementation of the agreed policies and programmes;

(c) to assist the principal officials in acquiring and deploying resources to support the implementation of policies and delivery of services;

(d) to monitor the needs and aspirations of the community and having regard to the findings, to undertake timely review and to generate proposals for necessary changes to the established policies and services;

(e) to uphold the reliability and professional standards in the delivery of services by the executive departments and agencies; and

(f) to ensure proper use of financial resources within the bureau and manage civil servants and other staff in the bureau.[48]

More generally:

The Secretaries of Department and Directors of Bureau will be directly responsible to the Chief Executive and they will have direct access to the Chief Executive. They will take part directly in the decision making process relating to the allocation of resources of the Government as a whole. They will have a strong say in the assignment of personnel working directly under them and the share of financial resources allocated to them.[49]

Executive Council

Under the Basic Law, the Executive Council is an organ for assisting the chief executive in policy-making. The council normally meets once a week, but sometimes more, or less, frequently. The chief executive presides over its meetings. Except for the appointment, removal and disciplining of officials and the adoption of measures in emergencies, the chief executive is obliged to consult the Executive Council before making important policy decisions, introducing bills to the Legislative Council, making subordinate legislation, or dissolving the Legislative Council.

If the chief executive does not accept a majority opinion of the Executive Council, he is required to put the specific reasons on record. However, the proceedings of the Executive Council are confidential. Members tender their advice individually, but the council's conclusions are presented as collective decisions.

Article 55 of the Basic Law stipulates that the chief executive shall appoint members of the Executive Council from among the principal officials of the executive authorities, members of the Legislative Council and public figures. With the implementation of the Accountability System for Principal Officials from 1 July 2002, the membership of the Executive Council now comprises the 14 principal officials appointed under the Accountability System and 15 non-officials.[50] Members' appointment or removal is decided by the chief executive. They have to be Chinese citizens who are permanent residents of the Hong Kong with no right of abode in any foreign country. They hold office for a period no longer than the expiry of the term of office of the chief executive who appoints them, but can be reappointed.

The new arrangement has probably made the council more unwieldy as a forum, and there have been suggestions that the number of official members should be cut back, with lower-ranking officials attending only when topics within their remit are being discussed.

The non-official members predominantly have backgrounds in the professions or financial sector. At least in the sphere of economic policy, this may ensure a measure of personal detachment by the majority from issues likely to come under discussion.

Legislative Council

The Legislative Council's primary function is to enact laws. There are, however, checks and balances between the executive authorities and the legislature. The Basic Law[51] provides that, if the chief executive considers that a bill passed by the Legislative Council is not compatible with the overall interests of Hong Kong and returns it to the Legislative Council for reconsideration, and if the original bill is passed by the Legislative Council again by not less than a two-thirds majority of all the members, the chief executive must sign and promulgate it within one month; or he may dissolve the Legislative Council. But if the original bill is then passed by the new Legislative Council by not less than a two-thirds majority of all the members, the chief executive must sign and promulgate it, or resign. The extent of autonomy of the HKSAR in making its own laws is set out under Article 17 of the Basic Law. Any laws that are enacted must be reported to the Standing Committee of the National People's Congress for the record. If (but only if) the Standing Committee, after consulting the Committee for the Basic Law of the HKSAR under it, considers that a law is not in conformity with the provisions of the Basic Law regarding affairs within the responsibility of the Central Authorities or regarding the relationship between the Central Authorities and the region, the Standing Committee may return the law in question but shall not amend it. Any law returned is immediately invalidated, but the invalidation has no retroactive effect.

Subject to these checks and balances, the Legislative Council has the ultimate authority to legislate. However, this does not amount to a fully democratic legislative process, since only half of the legislative councillors (30 out of 60 for the 2004–08 term of the Legislative Council) have been elected by universal suffrage; the remainder come from the functional constituencies. The 30 functional constituencies represent a broad spectrum of economic and social sectors, but largely covering producer interests rather than consumer interests.[52]

Aside from lawmaking, the Legislative Council has the following functions or powers:

- to examine and approve budgets introduced by the government
- to approve taxation and public expenditure
- to receive and debate the policy addresses of the chief executive
- to raise questions on the work of the government
- to debate any issue concerning the public interest

- to endorse the appointment and removal of judges of the Court of Final Appeal and the chief judge of the High Court
- to receive and handle complaints from Hong Kong residents
- to summon, as required when exercising the above-mentioned powers and functions, persons concerned to testify or give evidence
- impeachment of the chief executive.[53]

Although it possesses little by way of formal authority to originate policy, the Legislative Council has developed as an increasingly effective channel for expressing views to government and hence steering policy. Even though a motion, even if passed, may not formally bind the government in any way, government will not in practice persist with a policy in defiance of the majority view in the Council.

A study of the contribution of the functional constituency system to economic policy during the 2000–04 period concluded that, because these constituencies were heavily weighted to business interests, the system tended to reinforce the voice of business, which was already well represented by the Liberal Party (see below). It follows that LegCo as a whole is skewed towards business. The study concluded that this has tended to press the government, or encourage it, to be more interventionist in its economic policies, in a manner broadly favouring business, than might otherwise have been the case.[54]

Table 7.1   2004 Legislative Council election results

	Parties	Geographical constituencies*	Functional constituencies	Total seats
'Pro-Government'	Democratic Party	7	2	9
	Article 45 Concern Group	3	1	4
	Hong Kong Association for Democracy and People's Livelihood	1		1
	Hong Kong Confederation of Trade Unions	1		1
	Neighbourhood and Workers Service Centre	1		1
	The Frontier	1		1
	Other	4	4	8
'Pro-Government'	Democratic Alliance for Betterment of Hong Kong	8	4	12
	Liberal Party	2	8	10
	Hong Kong Federation of Trade Unions	1		1
	Other	1	11	12
Total		30	30	60

* Turnout rate in geographical constituencies, 55.6%

Political parties

It has been customary among the media and other observers to characterise parties and legislative councillors as either pro-democracy or pro-government (often assumed to be synonymous with pro-Beijing). This demarcation implies that the government is anti-democracy, which is false. However, since the labels are in popular usage, they are repeated here. In fact, many on the 'pro government' side favour democracy as an eventual goal, in the sense of universal suffrage on a conventional one-man-one-vote basis (as opposed to the mixed functional and geographic basis), and even Beijing acknowledges that the Basic Law provides for progress in that direction; the disagreement is over the pace at which it should be attained.

In the September 2004 elections 62% of the geographic constituency votes cast went to so-called pro-democracy candidates. The allocation of seats is shown in Table 7.1.

Economic policies of the parties

For the purposes of this study it is the contribution of the political parties to economic policy which is of interest.

The **Democratic Party**, whose main platform has been the pursuit of greater democracy in Hong Kong, proclaims little more than generalisations in the economics field. Thus:

> Hong Kong's economic prosperity is based on free trade, abundant productive human capital and an open policy towards foreign investment. Hong Kong needs to consolidate its status as a financial and trade centre in order to maintain the confidence of local and international investors in long term investment. This will maintain Hong Kong's prosperity, stability and growth.
>
> The Democratic Party considers the principle of fair competition to be compatible with principles of social justice and economic efficiency. When the free market fails to provide suitable conditions for free competition automatically, the Government should step in to ensure that economic and social development receive equal attention.
>
> To ensure continuous economic growth, the Hong Kong Government should not only maintain free market competition and the rule of law, but also improve infrastructure, the dissemination of information

and labour quality, as well as contain inflation. Such actions will create favourable conditions for Hong Kong's economic growth.

Hong Kong's economic development strategy should be conducive to mutual economic development between Hong Kong and the Mainland.[55]

The **Article 45 Concern Group** was established by a group of lawyers in LegCo, with a specific focus on constitutional and legal matters. In March 2006 it broadened itself out into a new formal political party, the **Civic Party**. Its foremost declared aim is "to promote democracy and social justice". It is also "committed to making Hong Kong an economic success, and that means better quality of life and better opportunities for everyone, sustainable development, healthy environment and rich cultural life." Thus far, the party or its key members have commented from time to time on economic issues, such as favouring action to promote competition, but have not promulgated any comprehensive economic strategy.

The **Hong Kong Association for Democracy and People's Livelihood** focuses mainly on grassroots concerns, such as income redistribution, health and education.

The **Frontier Party** is keenly committed on livelihood issues, where it adopts a fairly socialist stance, demanding better labour protection, such as legislation for minimum wages and maximum working hours, better social welfare and a reduction of rents in public housing estates. On the broader economic front, it has been pressing for a competition policy in Hong Kong to curb anti-competitive and monopolistic practices.

The **Democratic Alliance for the Betterment and Progress of Hong Kong** (DAB) is regarded first and foremost as the main pro-Beijing party. Recently it has become more adventurous in criticism of government, and has been strongly espousing 'green' policies. A flavour of its economic philosophy, which veers towards the interventionist, can be gleaned from its published platform:

> Hong Kong's distinguished position as an international financial, trade and service center depends on many factors. Hong Kong's well-established infrastructure, advanced communication facilities, sound financial system, industrious and zealous workforce and entrepreneurs who operate with remarkable flexibility and adaptability all play a vital role in Hong Kong's long-standing economic success.
>
> However, Hong Kong is faced with various problems including its exorbitant land prices, relatively high labor cost and its neglect of industrial

development. We must pay close attention to these challenges and work hard in coming up with effective solutions to real problems.

The return to China in 1997 has brought Hong Kong many opportunities and promise of economic development. Hong Kong must hold on to the very strengths that have contributed to its economic successful in the past. We must sharpen our competitive edge and equip ourselves with new tools for economic success and security. Hong Kong must take advantage of the benefits of China's rapidly growing and evolving economy by working closely with the Mainland to make full use of each other's strengths and promote prosperity in both lands.[56]

The statement continues with a wish-list, including more proactive industrial policies in the fields of industry and technology; better cooperation with the Mainland; measures (though not in any specific terms) to strengthen service industries, promote innovation, foster lifelong learning and worker training; a higher proportion of GDP devoted to education; support for SMEs; improved urban planning; steps to modulate land prices and make more land available.

The **Liberal Party** is regarded as the party of business interests, and individual members have often been strong advocates of government intervention to support particular sectors. However, as a party its economic philosophy is stated in only the most general terms:

> Economic and social progress for Hong Kong's people is the primary and perennial target to which we must all dedicate our efforts. We will strive for an even better future by sustained dynamic growth through sound economic principles and planning. Building on proven success, we aim to create an economy that will bring about jobs and wealth for all. In addition, we must, through long term planning, ensure that the growth we seek will be a sustainable one and that our children enjoy the best education so that they remain competitive in this increasingly globalised economy. We must constantly look to the future, welcome new technologies, adapt to innovative industries, and emulate leading trends in international trade. Our resources must be used cost-effectively and efficiently, and we must provide for social justice in line with our economic progress.
>
> As a community, we must help those members of our society who are unable to help themselves. As a multi-faceted economy relying on a full range of service industries upon which our GDP output is predominantly based, priorities must be given to the further improvement of Hong Kong's investment environment in order to enhance our global and regional competitiveness. The upholding of the principles for a level

playing field, and transparency in government, have become the prerequisites in our bid to achieve economic growth.[57]

The two trade union parties, the **Hong Kong Confederation of Trade Unions** and the **Hong Kong Federation of Trade Unions,** are each committed primarily to fighting for the rights and interests of workers. However, they are at opposite ends of the spectrum on constitutional issues, with the Confederation opposing the current political system as anti-democratic, while the Federation emphasises patriotism and loyalty to Beijing.

It is apparent from the above analysis that none of the political parties has yet articulated a comprehensive and coherent economic strategy in any but the most superficial terms. That deficiency was particularly apparent in the last round of Legislative Council elections and there are few signs of any clearer manifestos since then.

Nevertheless the emergence of the parties has helped to raise political awareness among the general public and provided a catalyst and self-confidence for individuals and interest groups to air their views and, in a number of cases, take to the streets in support of or protest against particular policies. This 'people power' has been perhaps the most significant development on the political front in recent years, and may be seen as inevitable within a society where basic rights to elect government are denied. In the context of the evolution of parties, one has witnessed increased activity by parties on particular single policy issues, especially where there is a clear popular interest. On the broader front, however, one senses that the public is left with only rather hazy perceptions about a party being 'pro-business', 'pro-grassroots', 'pro-democracy', 'pro-government' or 'pro-Beijing', but little idea as to what such supposed allegiances mean in terms of specific policy measures.

Two further organisations of a political nature deserve mention in this section for the sake of completeness, although neither can really be classed as a political party in Hong Kong.

First, the **Hong Kong Alliance in Support of Patriotic Democratic Movements of China** is a pro-democratic organization that was established in 1989 with the purpose of supporting democracy, human rights and the release of dissidents in China. It is known most visibly for its support for yearly commemorations in Hong Kong of the Tiananmen Square massacre of 1989. It does not play any significant part in economic debate.

The final mention goes to the **National Committee of the Chinese**

People's Political Consultative Conference (CPPCC). There are around 200 Hong Kong delegates on the Committee, appointed by the Mainland authorities, a number of whom are also members of the election committee for Hong Kong's chief executive. Recently, the CPPCC and some of its provincial chapters have established fraternity associations in Hong Kong. Although this is presented as a mechanism for allowing Hong Kong people more voice in national politics, it is regarded by some as a means for infiltrating Mainland influence into Hong Kong politics, and hence as a potential threat to Hong Kong's independence under the one-country-two-systems arrangement.

Central Policy Unit

Within Hong Kong, the chief executive is the ultimate arbiter of policies. In addition to the statutory role of the Executive Council in advising him, he can take advice from the Central Policy Unit (CPU).

The CPU came into being in 1989 and retained its structure after 1997. But, whereas prior to 1997 it was prominent in providing intellectual leadership on policy issues, since 1997 it appears to have been on the wane, and has now been displaced from its senior status by the Commission on Strategic Development.

Its major declared function is to provide advice on policy matters to the chief executive and his two leading subordinates, the chief secretary for administration and the financial secretary. Its establishment includes a number of researchers and supporting personnel from diverse backgrounds. In addition, the CPU can draw on some 50 part-time members from different sectors. It also commissions specific consultancy studies from relevant experts. And it represents Hong Kong in discussions with Guangdong organisations and in research studies in support of Hong Kong/Guangdong cooperation. It is titularly responsible for coordinating the drafting of the chief executive's annual policy address. It occasionally organises public forums to focus attention on issues of supposed public concern, but there were only two such events in 2005 and one in 2006.

Judging from the CPU's own propaganda,[58] one might expect it to be the key strategy originator in Hong Kong. But a look at the list of members of the unit and its advisers, and at its published output, reveals that little by way of key economic thought has emerged from this source.

Its main preoccupation appears to lie with "Socio-Economic-Political Trends in Pan-Pearl River Delta Region" on which it has published a long list of consultancy reports. It has also published studies on the role of Hong Kong's so-called third sector — voluntary and non-profit organisations. But there is very little in these two topics to guide the major strategies of economic policy; they scarcely represent a portfolio of key policy issues of the sort which one might expect a senior advisory unit to be addressing.

Advisory bodies

In part because of the absence of democracy, and as a means of introducing outside views to government and instigating a measure of accountability, a huge network of advisory committees has built up over a long period.

Their intended function is evident from this quote from the chief executive:[59]

> At present, the Government has a few hundred advisory boards and statutory bodies. They serve as important partners in achieving effective governance. We attach great importance to the work they do. We see them as think-tanks for public policies and channels for our people to participate in public affairs. When current members' terms expire, we will actively seek to bring in more people from different sectors. They will be able to participate and give play to their talent in helping the Government take the public pulse and improve governance. I will pay particular attention to the participation of women, young people and the disadvantaged.

Another government source provides a bit more detail:

> The network of advisory . . . bodies is a distinctive feature of the system of government. It seeks to obtain, through consultation with interested groups and individuals in the community, the best possible advice on which to base decisions or to perform statutory functions. . . . Some of the advisory bodies, such as the Telecommunications Standards Advisory Committee, deal with the interests of a particular industry. Others advise on a particular area of government policy interest, such as the Transport Advisory Committee. Some advisory bodies, such as the District Fire Safety Committees and Area Committees, deal essentially with district affairs. Government officials and members of the public are represented on these bodies. About 6,000 members of the public have been appointed to serve on around 500 bodies, and some serve on more than one. These people

are appointed in view of their specialist knowledge or expertise, their record or interest in contributing to community service, and the specific needs of the concerned bodies.[60]

On studying the terms of reference of the advisory committees and, where they are available, the agendas or minutes of their meetings, it is apparent that in the overwhelming majority of cases their role is to advise on the implementation of policies, or monitor the implementation, rather than to formulate or propose policies in the first place. Despite government urgings that the advisory bodies should be as transparent as possible in their deliberations, although most of them provide information over the internet about their formal role and membership, few release substantive material about their deliberations.[61] And, in some instances at least, any involvement of these bodies in policy formation is likely to have been diluted or edged out completely by the recently fortified Commission on Strategic Development.

Following a recommendation from the Legislative Council in 2000, the administration set in train a review of the roles and functions of statutory bodies and advisory committees. Thus far, the review process has resulted in a good deal of exhortation about the significance and value of the system, and some tinkering at the edges (e.g. efforts to widen the scope of membership and limit terms of office), but there have neither been very fundamental changes nor visible evidence that the various committees are functioning any more effectively.

Historically, the system has served at best as a means of building consensus, but at worst, through judicious selection of members and official guidance of agendas, as a means of conferring legitimacy on the preferred policies of the administration. Nowadays, the public demands greater transparency and accountability, and is prepared to mount open challenges to government policies. If the committee system cannot adapt to these needs, its relevance may further diminish.

Commission on Strategic Development

The Commission on Strategic Development deserves space here, not so much for any achievements so far in its eight-year existence, as for the fact that the present chief executive has declared it to be the most important advisory body. It was originally established in 1998 to explore the way forward for

Hong Kong's long-term development strategies. In 2002 it produced a report on long-term development goals, which contained exhortatory rhetoric about a "holistic long-term strategy", the "knowledge-based economy", "embracing new technologies", "enhancing the quality of the environment" and "strengthening the social fabric". And it identified four fairly obvious and uncontentious themes as important for Hong Kong to focus upon: Mainland opportunities, competitiveness, quality of life and — a telling one, in the light of Chapter 2 — image projection to the outside world.

Subsequently, however, little or nothing was heard of the commission, and it effectively lay dormant. That was until October 2005, when the new chief executive, Donald Tsang, relaunched it. He announced in his policy address that he looked upon the commission as Hong Kong's most important advisory body, and that he would substantially expand its membership by inviting talent from different fields.

The role of the commission, as now stated, is to serve as a platform for all sectors of the community to explore with the government major issues pertaining to Hong Kong's long-term development. The intention is to gauge a wide range of community views at the early stage of policy formulation to be considered by the relevant policy bureaus, thereby laying the foundation for formulating specific policies. The commission's work is intended to make policy formulation more scientific and transparent, backed up by enhanced public participation and acceptance.

Four committees were then set up within the commission: an "Executive Committee", a "Committee on Governance and Political Development", a "Committee on Social Development and Quality of Life" and a "Committee on Economic Development and Economic Cooperation with the Mainland". Each committee comprises a small number of senior government officials together with 35 to 40 non-officials.

The commission and its four committees are served by a secretariat established within the Central Policy Unit (CPU), which provides both secretarial and research support. It appears that, both in terms of its place in the policy formation process and its demands on the CPU's resources, the commission has upstaged the CPU itself and further eclipsed whatever meagre influence the CPU may have had.

The commission has already sought to make an impact, but by word rather than deed. As regards matters specifically on the economic front, it produced the following desiderata under the heading of economic development at its first meeting in November 2005:[62]

- enhance Hong Kong's economic competitiveness
- position as a "knowledge-based" economy focusing on the delivery of world-class services
- better leverage on the Mainland's economic development
- further facilitate the interflow of capital, talent, goods, information and people between the Mainland and Hong Kong
- adjust developmental strategies in line with China's Eleventh Five-Year Plan
- import talent from the Mainland and abroad
- invest heavily in higher education and research
- increase language proficiency
- serve as a major medical centre in China and the East Asian Region
- "export" legal and financial services to the Mainland and abroad
- provide a better business environment by cutting the "costs" imposed by government and bureaucracy, and adopting business-friendly tax regime
- promote sports and creative industries

Also relevant to economic policy were some of the views expressed under the heading of social development, *viz*:
- pay more attention to the low value-added part of the "dual economy"
- address mismatch in the labour market
- review the land policy so that it would not hamper economic growth and create social inequities
- study the issues arising from increasing income inequality such as the polarization within the middle class, minimum wage, standard working hours, etc.
- pay more attention to social groups facing serious hardship and deserving particular attention, e.g. disadvantaged children and youth
- address the problem of ageing population
- ensure social stability which is essential to sustained economic and political development
- provide more support for the family
- establish a Commission on Children
- strengthen the cohesion of "The Third Side" to maintain social stability and harmony, and to serve as a bridge between the people of Hong Kong and the Central Authorities
- instill more sense of pride and responsibility to the motherland
- better protect the environment

Since this book is concerned with the process of policy formation as much as with its substance, it is also worth noting the commission's declared aims in that same document in the field of political development, *viz*:

- achieve strong and effective governance
- review the present political structure to better define the division of powers between the executive and the legislature
- encourage development of political parties, particularly a "government" party
- better engage the community in the discussion of public policies; better manage public demands for social and public services to narrow the gap between public demands and fiscal capacity
- pursue democratic development in accordance with the Basic Law and having regard to Hong Kong's prosperity and stability; build a Hong Kong-style democracy featuring openness and fairness
- ensure stability and coherence of public policies, which are essential to maintaining stability amidst dramatic social and economic changes
- provide opportunities for the "silent majority" to come out with their views in order to promote political moderation and "harmony"

These lists provide a potentially exciting, though perhaps suffocatingly long, range of issues. However, the commission's membership, as reconstituted, was coterminous with the chief executive's appointment — i.e. only to June 2007. It has therefore decided to confine the commission's activities to a small number of issues, with the prospect of making worthwhile progress to that time horizon. They were, in descending order of priority:

- Hong Kong's positioning in our country's economic, social and political development
- Hong Kong's positioning in the international community and international affairs
- Hong Kong's international competitiveness
- balanced and sustainable development on all fronts

This may be a worthy list, and the obeisance to Beijing in the first one may also be noted, but they are so general as to be unlikely to produce any pathbreaking ideas. Moreover, it seems extraordinary that a commission, explicitly mandated to tackle long-term issues, has not felt able to embark on work which would extend beyond the assured term of office of its current members.

Meanwhile, the commission's economic committee has been charged with pursuing the following topics:

- promoting the development of creative industries
- Hong Kong as a hub for talent
- high value-added logistics
- creation of employment[63]

These are rather more specific, but the list hints at a 'picking winners' mentality, and suggests that government may have a direct role in creating jobs — an attitude which is at variance with Hong Kong's longstanding approach to running the economy.

Whether the commission can make a meaningful contribution to policy remains to be seen. Not everyone can monitor progress, since the briefings after each committee meeting are issued only in Chinese. One suspects that the unwieldy structure and the large numbers of people involved may militate against any very speedy delivery. That suspicion appears to be borne out by the fact that at the time of writing — a good 18 months since the commission's relaunch — the "Researches and Studies" page of its website remains blank.

Commission on Poverty

In February 2005 a Commission on Poverty was established under the chairmanship of the financial secretary, comprising government officials, Legislative Councillors, business people, non-government organisations, experts and academics. It was charged to:

- study and identify the needs of the poor
- make policy recommendations to alleviate poverty and promote self-reliance
- encourage community engagement; delineate responsibility between the government, social welfare sector and community organisations; foster public-private partnerships and mobilise social capital in alleviating poverty

The aim was to provide a forum for different sectors of the community to work together to study and explore practical ways to help the poor in terms of their financial, employment, education and training needs.[64] The commission's report (not yet available at the time of writing) has indeed been expected to focus intelligently on issues at the community, workplace and educational levels. But the commission was steered away from key macroeconomic aspects, such as the overall welfare budget, housing policy, and taxation, which are highly relevant in the context of the rich-poor divide. It is unlikely that major inroads can be made into poverty without there being significant budgetary implications. The battlelines would then be clear between those who believe most firmly in self-help and minimal government intervention, and those who are disposed to a more generous official provision of a social safety net.

Council of international advisers

Tung Chee Hwa, while he was chief executive, established a council of international advisers which, during his terms of office, met once a year in Hong Kong. According to the official announcement, it was formed to keep the administration abreast of key global issues which might affect Hong Kong. Quite apart from the fact that it may have been insulting to many locals that pride of place should be given to foreign businessmen in reaching the chief executive's ear on economic policy, there was no evidence, from seven years of meetings, of the council ever having offered any serious advice. Rather, the members seemed to offer banal observations about the world, and then pat the Hong Kong government on the back with an endorsement of this or that aspect of policy. It was more suggestive of a body assembled to boost spirits and ego, and provide comforting reassurance, than a serious exercise in policy advice. Whilst some international advice and comment may be helpful, if it comes exclusively from businessmen — no environmentalists, educationalists, economists or the like — it is bound to be biased, and likely to produce essentially what a fellow businessman, or ex-businessman as Tung was, would be most comforted to hear.

A flavour of the 'advice' so tendered can be found in the press releases that followed each meeting. Thus, in November 2003:

> They acknowledged that the surge in Asia-Pacific's intra-regional exports signified its rising importance in world trade. They were also of the view that Hong Kong, with the implementation of CEPA and its further economic integration with the Pearl River Delta, would play an increasingly important role in channelling trade between the Mainland and the other Asia-Pacific economies. They endorsed Hong Kong's strategy of economic development. They agreed that Hong Kong should position itself as a regional service centre and continue to harness its competitive advantages while upgrading the value added in its services.

And, in November 2004,

> They discussed the opportunities and challenges the global and regional developments were bringing to Hong Kong, in particular Hong Kong's role in the development of the Greater Pearl River Delta (PRD) and Pan-PRD. . . . members had an in-depth and productive exchange of views on the developments in the Greater PRD and Pan-PRD, the global and regional economic outlook, the energy market in particular oil prices, international trade and monetary issues as well as their impact on Hong Kong. During the second session of the meeting in Guangzhou, the Guangdong Governor, Mr Huang Huahua, gave a comprehensive briefing on Guangdong's latest economic performance, Hong Kong–Guangdong co-operation and the opportunities presented by developments in the Greater PRD and Pan-PRD.

Significantly, the current chief executive, Donald Tsang, decided not to proceed with a planned meeting of the panel in November 2005, perhaps through potential embarrassment at how few members might have turned up, or at the vast expense involved, or perhaps simply because the body was very much the personal creation of his predecessor, for which he had much less enthusiasm. Moreover, the year 2006 passed without any sign or sound of the council. One may reasonably conclude that it has been allowed to wither.

Commissioned reports and consultancies

Another channel of policy formulation comprises commissioned studies and consultancies. The government makes liberal use of these, in proper acknowledgement that certain areas of expertise are not available within the civil service. Interestingly, these exercises probably play a greater role in bringing key policy proposals to the table than do most of the advisory committees. The feasibility of further railway lines on Hong Kong Island, or of a new container terminal, the strategic direction of banking in Hong Kong, options for the financing and delivery of health care and the broadening of the tax base, all serve as examples.

While there is plainly a need to draw on outside expertise in this way, there is also a danger of the consultancy process being used merely to rubber stamp ideas on which the administration is keen, rather providing an entirely objective view of the choices available. The instance of Cyberport has already been mentioned in Chapter 3. And studies commissioned on privatisation of the airport authority and on the need for a deposit insurance scheme were, given the known leanings of the authorities in favour of the ideas in both instances, and given that many of those interviewed in the consultation process may have had vested interests in the projects going ahead, less likely to have played a part in actually determining the direction of policy, than in validating a chosen policy for the eyes of the public.

Consulting the public, and the public expressing itself

An important element in the gestation of policy is the public consultation process. In 2005 alone, for example, the government launched formal consultation exercises on a mixture of topics that included: reforms to secondary and higher education; exemption of offshore funds from profits tax; duty on alcohol; a concept plan for Lantau; privatisation of the Airport Authority; regulation of fishing; listing requirements on the stock exchange; green tourism; the electricity market; and development of the west Kowloon cultural district. These were followed in 2006 by consultations on private redevelopment; domestic rent policy; the future of the district councils; competition policy; radio spectrum licensing; the development of the political appointment system; and tax reform.

Consultations of this sort are common the world over as a means of fine-tuning the details of laws and regulations, identifying inconsistencies or impracticalities, making them workable or, in some circumstances, hastening their abandonment. But in most cases the general premise is that the government or the lawmakers have decided upon the broad sweep of a particular policy, and have the backing of their democratic mandate to press forward with that, and are now asking the public to assist them in bringing the policy into effect as efficiently and sensibly as possible.

In Hong Kong, however, consultation has also evolved, in some instances, as a means of marshalling public support for a policy — a sort of ersatz democracy. The potential difficulty then is what to do if the weight of response is opposed to the policy. A concentration of opposition, whether informed or ill-informed, may, if it gains sufficient momentum, run the risk of derailing even some very necessary and, to most people's minds, reasonable measures, even if supported by the establishment, including the Legislative Council. The opposition may not be massive. The administration has sometimes run scared and abandoned policies simply on account of opposition from a vocal minority and in fear of street demonstrations or the like if it persisted. For instance, the proposal for a land border crossing levy came to a halt in 2002 for that sort of reason, and has never since seen the light of day, despite being, in many respects, a very sensible, fair and efficient fiscal measure. By contrast, in a democracy, an administration might feel that it had the legitimacy to press ahead with its plans nonetheless.

The formal consultation procedure in Hong Kong is designed, among other things, to try to pre-empt populist reactionism and megaphone populism. It may well succeed, provided that the government is honest about consulting and therefore willing to digest the comments received and adjust policy accordingly. A willingness to do so does not mean that every counterproposal which carries a simple majority must automatically be acted upon, since the response process is sure to be biased in various ways. But the comments need to receive a proper, considered response. It was the government's alleged attempts to massage, in its favour, the presentation of results from the consultation process, launched in December 2002, over the proposals to implement article 23 of the Basic Law (concerning security matters) that aroused public outrage and led to the famous pro-democracy rally of 1 July 2003, subsequent to which the government, fearful of any further such consequences, shelved the subject for the time being.

Since then, the public demonstration has become a common means to air public opinion on controversial issues. It is, of course, a tactic used the world over to vent opinion and, most commonly, to oppose government policies. The difference for Hong Kong is that the government is not in a position to say that there is democratic authority behind its policies. Other things being equal, it may therefore feel obliged to take rather more notice of such expressions of public opinion than would governments in other jurisdictions.

In parallel to the visible consultation process, there are occasional signs of less transparent methods. In May 2006, for example, the chief executive came under fire for not revealing the nature of a survey which, he claimed, demonstrated that 70% of the public supported the government's plans for the construction of new government offices on the Tamar site. There are also suspicions that 'consultation' too often takes place behind closed doors with any of a small coterie of leading business figures (of which more in Chapter 8).

In sum, for Hong Kong the procedure of consultation and encouragement of public debate may help the political process, but it can also be damaging if opposition, especially when vocal or visible, is allowed to prevail despite not representing majority opinion.

Lobby groups independent of government

There was a time when it would have been fair to say that Hong Kong lacked any bodies which possessed the intellectual calibre or presentational skills to make a mark in analysing or challenging the economic policies emanating from the government and its inner circle. Traditional organisations such as the chambers of commerce were unlikely to cause serious upsets. In recent years, however, the landscape has been changing.

Chambers of commerce

Historically, the principal visible interest groups in Hong Kong were the chambers of commerce, of which there are many, representing both Hong Kong businesses and foreign businesses operating in the territory. But these are first and foremost associations committed to representing their own members. They do produce comments on policy proposals and advice on technical details, as well as guidance to the government about their likely acceptability and potential impact. But, apart from the pre-budget submissions which some of them offer, and which comprise a wish list of the business lobby rather than considered strategic insights, they are essentially reactive rather than proactive in terms of economic policy in the broad sense. The Hong Kong General Chamber of Commerce perhaps carries the greatest weight as the voice of the business establishment, while the Chinese Chamber of Commerce is seen by its critics as too ready to proffer unquestioning support for the administration and too ready to be seen as supinely loyal to Beijing.

Generally speaking, the narrower is the membership constituency of any group, the narrower, understandably, is their area of focus. Thus, the myriad of other business organisations make even less of a contribution to questions of broad economic strategy than do the more widely drawn chambers of commerce.

Universities

Despite the steady growth of universities in Hong Kong over the years, there has tended to be surprisingly little contribution from relevant academic departments to the macroeconomic policy debate. There are no individuals or academic groups to which the administration can look for a steady stream of research, analysis or debate on contemporary policy issues. This is not to deny that individual academics may occasionally voice their views on particular issues, or be involved in consultancy or advisory work for the government or official bodies when invited to do so. Nor is it to deny that some economics departments make valuable contributions to the economic debate — such as the University of Hong Kong's Centre for Economic Research which publishes regular economic forecasts and, from time to time, papers which make a material contribution on policy issues such as housing. But those contributions are rather infrequent. There is no unit that could be described as keeping the government continuously on its toes by carrying out day-to-day scrutiny of the evolution of economic policy and making continuous original contributions to it.

Think-tanks

Partly, in the run-up to the handover of sovereignty to China, as a reflection of anxiety over the way in which Hong Kong might be run after 1997, and partly, in more recent years, in recognition of the need for independent policy analysis to keep the administration on its toes and in some instances to challenge the traditional government-business alliance, a number of think-tanks have been formed. These are described in the following paragraphs, in chronological order of foundation.

The **Hong Kong Democratic Foundation**[65] dates from 1989. Essentially, it represents business and professional people sympathetic to democratic ideals. The tone is liberal rather than distinctly radical. Thus:

> Government involvement in the economy should be kept to a minimum. However, government needs to play a role in maintaining and promoting industrial standards, regulating essential monopolies, ensuring free and fair competition and creating an economic environment that allows business to operate under uniform regulations and share equal access to information and market opportunities. Government should provide the necessary

services and the physical and intellectual infrastructure. It should also encourage private sector participation in providing these, while ensuring accountability to the people. Free enterprise and the right to private ownership are essential ingredients of our free-market economy. They must be maintained along with those policies that have made Hong Kong an important international commercial and financial centre.

The Foundation has remained consistent in its philosophy, but, beyond such general statements of support for Hong Kong's traditional values, has had little influence over the formulation of policy.

The **Business and Professionals Federation of Hong Kong**[66] was formed in 1990. It is a group of business and professional people who declare a common goal of stability and prosperity for Hong Kong. It has published various pieces of research, in the hope of influencing public policy makers. In the economic sphere the subjects have included health care reform and broadening of the tax base. Although not strikingly original in its positions, the fact that the Federation makes the effort to conduct analysis rather than just spout rhetoric, and the establishment nature of its membership, have at least ensured it a hearing in the policy debate.

The **Hong Kong Policy Research Institute**[67] was set up by a small group of business, professional and academic people in 1995, aiming to deliver policy research relevant to "the long-term development of Hong Kong and of the Chinese community", and based on the following principles:

- to promote the development of Hong Kong based on the concept of "One Country, Two Systems" and the premise of Hong Kong's return to China
- to take into consideration the development of Greater China
- to liaise with neighbouring governments and related research institutions
- to take root in the community, promoting public discussion on social policies, and proposing forward-looking ideas which are independent of the government and of political parties
- to be "non-partisan", "non-pressure group type", and "non-profit-making" in nature, and to be a policy research institution receiving funding from commissioned research projects
- to maintain independence, openness and a high degree of transparency in research process and results

In practice the Institute has struggled somewhat to maintain any momentum and, while contributing in recent years to the debate on constitutional issues, has made little impact in the field of economic policy.

The **Better Hong Kong Foundation**[68] also dates from 1995. It was the brainchild of 21 leading local business and community leaders, concerned about emerging misconceptions in the international community regarding Hong Kong's future, and intent on enhancing confidence — both economic and social — in Hong Kong. It lays emphasis on the continuity of the philosophy and policies which made Hong Kong a success in the past, and is therefore fairly conservative and, in its pronouncements on economic policy, generally supportive of the administration. Its views tend to carry some weight because its members include many of the senior business establishment, though the views themselves tend not to differ significantly from those of other business-based groups. It is one of the more active think-tanks — for example sponsoring discussion of Hong Kong's competitiveness and commissioning research specifically into its competitiveness as a sea-logistics hub.

The **Social and Economic Policy Institute**[69] was founded in January 2000 by a group of academics, researchers and trade unionists, wanting to broaden the public debate on the social impacts of social and economic policies. As that suggests, the focus of its work is almost exclusively on social and labour issues.

The **Civic Exchange**[70] was also founded in 2000, "to promote civic education on economic, social and environmental issues; . . . and to undertake research on economic, social and political policies in the hope of helping to expand and improve the public policy debate on such issues." Of all the think-tanks the Exchange has probably sustained the greatest influence and made the greatest substantive contribution to policy debates. This is partly because of shrewd public relations, but more substantively because it has produced in-depth and original research on a wide range of topics — to quote but a few examples, care of the environment, constitutional reform and, in more specifically economic fields, transport policy and budgetary accounting.

The **Lion Rock Institute**[71] was founded in 2004, by a couple of committed individuals, expressing a concern for the future of Hong Kong. As a voice that is passionate about preserving economic freedoms and strongly opposed to any creeping socialism, it plays a useful role in providing an intellectual challenge to any presumptions about the need for government involvement in the economy.

SynergyNet[72] was established in 2001 by a group of intellectuals and professionals coming from the academic, business, social service and political sectors, as "a forum for the exchange of ideas on policies and strategies affecting the long-term development of Hong Kong". In practice it has indeed mostly played that sort of journalistic role, rather than purporting to generate new ideas or research. And it seems to have become increasingly a one-man band.

The latest think-tank to arrive on the scene was the **Bauhinia Foundation**,[73] in March 2006. It is staffed and well funded by eminent persons who are known supporters of Chief Executive Donald Tsang, and was caricatured as a support organisation for securing his re-election in 2007. It has, however, launched, in collaboration with others, some seemingly worthwhile research projects — into issues such as competitiveness and health care. The nature of any policy prescriptions or strategies that may emerge from the research remains to be seen.

– 8 –

How Economic Policies Emerge

Democratic deficit

You do not have to be in Hong Kong for very long before you realise that there is something strange about the policy formation process, whether in economics or any other policy domain. Moreover, depending on what you read or whom you listen to, there is a mixture of frustration, embarrassment, resignation and even, among the establishment, a sort of collective guilt complex about it all. These mixed emotions arise essentially from the lack of democracy and from the opacity of the substitute procedures.

In the mature democracies of the world, it is clear that the ultimate sanction of policy rests with elected powers. Thus, in the United States the elected President has the mandate to appoint an administration around him and to rule with a constitutionally defined executive authority. In various matters he needs to obtain congressional approval. But, again, the Senate and the House of Representatives are elected bodies. In the United Kingdom the mandate to govern rests effectively with the prime minister, who heads the majority party elected to the House of Commons and who can usually therefore count upon parliamentary support for his decisions. Other countries range across the spectrum between the presidential and parliamentary systems. In all cases, however, economic policies, or any other, are set and executed by those who have a legitimate democratic mandate.

The way in which economic policy is formulated in those environments may vary greatly. It may be driven by party manifestos. It may filter upwards from skilful civil servants. It may reflect the personal agenda of the political leader, or a small group of politicians or cronies surrounding him or her. It may, especially as election dates draw near, acknowledge prevailing populist sentiment. More probably it will be a combination of these.

But the crucial factor in the democratic environment is that the electorate has the opportunity to kick the president or ruling party out of office at the end of their term. In the meantime they have the mandate to govern, and generally speaking they get on with that job.

Meanwhile, even though many people may acquiesce only reluctantly, or disapprovingly, to the policies and measures which are adopted — often the elected government will have been the first choice of fewer than half the voters — they are usually willing to accept and respect the governing mandate. Only rarely will opposition, resentment or emotions run so high as to provoke strong enough reactions to deflect the government from its chosen path.

All of that would be taken for granted by anyone living in such countries. Hong Kong is different. The lack of democracy results in sections of the community often being deeply sceptical about the motives, justification or wisdom of policies. In recognition of that and as a response to it, the administration nowadays falls over itself to try to achieve popular approval for all it does.

Origination of policies and the missing ingredient

Where do the ideas and initiatives for economic policy in Hong Kong come from, and how is it decided which ones shall proceed?

There is no very clear, definitive answer. The impression gained is that the government pays lip service to the tradition of a market-driven economy with minimal government interference — whether under the slogan of "positive non-interventionism" or "market leads, government facilitates" — and then devises policies on spending, taxation and so on, which are consistent with that philosophy. Civil servants, the Legislative Council, consultants and advisory committees and the like may all play some role in mapping out the detail. None of that is at all surprising or controversial.

It is extremely hard, however, as the discussion in the preceding chapter has proved, to identify any persons or groups within the institutional infrastructure that provide the intellectual leadership or play a clearly significant part in the formation of the economic strategies or policies. Civil servants prepare the papers which form the basis for the policy decisions taken by the chief executive after discussion in the Executive Council, but who originates the strategic direction? Is it top-down or bottom-up? Who actually inspires the idea and then makes the running for such diverse initiatives as, for example, Cyberport, a design centre, the Lantau cable car, a goods and services tax, the Science Park, the suspension or resumption of land sales, or a push to allow more Mainlanders to work in Hong Kong?

The answer is, of course, that there are many different routes to the table, which is perhaps why no single one is prominent. These have been catalogued in the previous chapter. But there is a missing ingredient from that catalogue. That is the somewhat nebulous concept of 'business interests'. Although business interests have been noted as being well represented and potentially influential in such groupings as the Liberal Party, the chambers of commerce, advisory committees and some think-tanks, none of these bodies exerts, of itself, an enormously powerful thrust on policy.

However, the business lobby, collectively, probably plays quite a weighty, yet subtle role, largely invisible and anonymous. Business leaders enjoy direct access to top officials, most importantly the chief executive and the financial secretary. Given that these officials are the ultimate arbiters of economic policy and frequently the instigators of any new initiatives, this access allows, in effect, the entire chain of advisers, legislators, committees, lobby groups and so forth to be short-circuited.

Of course, as noted in the earlier discussion, policies cannot nowadays, in practice, be imposed on a significantly unwilling public. But there are many areas of policy — the proposal for a logistics park may be cited as a current example — where the business lobby can be hugely influential in steering events while, at the same time, the issue is not one that is likely to engage a great deal of interest among the general public. Under such conditions, government measures, probably including some that are interventionist in all but name, can be slipped through with little opposition.

In many respects, this is nothing new for Hong Kong. Way back through the British colonial era, the administration depended considerably on both informal business contacts and on hand-picked appointees to the Executive Council from the business fraternity, who provided valuable technical input as well as advice on the community's reaction to policy proposals.

In that era, the civil service was at one with the governor, and the senior civil servants in the policy branches of the government secretariat did most of the policy work. London adopted a largely hands-off stance in matters of

Hong Kong's internal affairs, bowing to local opinion and the instincts of its appointed administrators — a detachment that is evidenced by the widening gulf for much of the period from 1945 to 1980 between the *laissez-faire* capitalism of Hong Kong and the socialist flirtations of the UK government at home. It was notable how senior civil servants, most of whom were British, showed such strong commitment to the Hong Kong model. Importantly also, the Hong Kong government seldom felt impelled to do something simply to curry favour with London. There is now much more of a tendency to kowtow to Beijing than there ever was to London. And in those days there was unlikely to be material opposition to policies from legislators, think-tanks or the general public, in the way that might all too readily spring up today.

One of the most important differences between then and now is that in colonial times the government could maintain a degree of detachment from the business lobby, despite relying on it for advice. Officials did not owe their positions to local businessmen, or hope for lucrative private sector employment after retirement from the civil service. Nowadays, the chief executive is himself elected by a process which gives considerable weight to the business establishment, while ever closer ties have been developing between business leaders and the Mainland authorities, who have ultimate sanction over senior government appointments. The power of business is also reinforced by the functional constituency system for the Legislative Council, where members nowadays exert a significantly stronger influence on policy than was the case when the Council was little more than an official rubber-stamping authority.

Now that principal officials are appointed with explicit responsibility for policy and are detached from the civil service, the former seamless interface between civil service and policy has been broken. Although the majority of principal officials are ex-civil servants, they are political creatures now. They are all members of the Executive Council, which has become an unwieldy body. Although its proceedings are not published, it is difficult to envisage broad strategic directions being set there. Meanwhile civil servants with no political aspirations, or who, for one reason or another, would not anyway be acceptable in the principal official posts, may have lost the urge to contribute to policy development. In short, there is now a disjuncture between policy initiatives on the one hand and the technical, unbiased skills of the civil service on the other. Members of the public, no longer confident that policies are being drawn up by politically neutral technocrats with Hong

Kong's best interests at heart, not personal ambition, have become sceptical and cynical about the entire policy process.

The colonial system involved a balance, often uneasy, between colonial bureaucrats and local business interests, whether foreign or locally owned. But the system ensured, in matters of personnel, a clear disconnect between the bureaucracy and business. The colonial bureaucracy had its own line of succession. As noted above, business interests were, undeniably, a powerful influence on the administration, and business might often have got its own way; but ultimately the government was always able to say no.

Now times have changed. Britain having failed to bequeath democracy as a replacement for its colonial procedures, Hong Kong is left with a system based too heavily on unhealthy links, often lacking transparency, between government and an unelected, quasi-hereditary business elite — the so-called 'tycoonocracy'.

The much vaunted slogan of "business-friendly government" is supposed to mean the provision of an attractive, fair and evenly competitive environment for all players, with proper but not excessive regulation. It should not extend, as it seems to have in Hong Kong, to embody persistent acquiescence to the special pleadings of individual businesses or businessmen. At that point it becomes, in practice, a breeding ground for the inefficient allocation of resources.

What is doubly damaging about the presence of the tycoonocracy is that it saps the interest and enthusiasm of other serious-minded persons in the context of contributing to the policy process. That is why appointees to advisory committees are caricatured as glancing at the papers in the car on the way to the meeting and then nodding in approval at proposals tabled by officials; they know that the real influence is wielded in other corridors of power. That is probably also a reason why it is only the most energetic and persevering individuals who can invigorate a think-tank beyond the luncheon-club-with-guest-speaker status.

Business interests and intervention

It is in part the strength of the business lobby's influence which has led to an apparent increase in the government's direct involvement in micro-managing the economy. One sector presses successfully for some favour. Others follow suit. None is prepared seriously to oppose the other; the principle of 'You scratch my back and I'll scratch yours' is plainly in play. Thus, we have seen government money put (or the opportunity to raise revenues foregone) into science parks, Cyberport and Disneyland. There is a hint of forthcoming support for a logistics park and a further container terminal. Policy and budget addresses talk of focusing on four key sectors — financial services, tourism, logistics, producer services — with a hint of doses of public money here and there. Then, for good measure and to satisfy a few more lobbyists, there is to be some help for creative and cultural activities, and for small and medium-sized businesses too.

The extent of government intervention should not, however, be exaggerated. Overall it is far less than in most other developed economies. Some of it is more exhortation and logistical support than monetary disbursement. And there is a fuzzy dividing line between the very necessary provision of public infrastructure and the subsidy to a particular business. But, since the end of the colonial era, the mentality seems to have shifted perceptibly to the idea that government has some sort of direct role to play in identifying key sectors (as, for example, explicitly announced in speeches) and rendering them some sort of support. In many cases, as noted earlier, support is manifest in the form of reducing the cost of land.

The mounting role of public opinion

If the insidious power of the business lobby is one distinctive aspect of policy formation in Hong Kong, a second is the role of public opinion. As noted already, because there is only limited electoral democracy, members of the public express their views through other channels. These are two sorts. One is the formal consultation process instituted by the government on specific proposals. The other is the meeting, rally or march, initiated by people and pressure groups themselves, usually in opposition to government plans.

The government desires to rule by consensus and is fearful of mass opposition and the possibility of civil unrest, not so much because it might be uncontrollable (there is no sign of that to date), as because officials realise that Beijing is concerned lest Mainland groups might copy such practices. Thus the government has become scared to enact any measures which might incite visible popular opposition. As a result, we have seen some perfectly reasonable budgetary proposals, such as a border-crossing levy, much needed increases in fees and charges for public services, and the goods and services tax, either dropped or pushed far into the future.

During British rule, successive financial secretaries seemed to be more forthright and self-confident in their decisions, whether good or bad, than have been their post-1997 successors. This may reflect the fact that in colonial times there was seldom any risk of vocal public opposition to government measures. Moreover, in those days, although officials were accountable for their policies in the literal sense of having to give answers in the Legislative Council, the questions came from generally friendly and compliant councillors. Officials did not have to regard themselves as formally accountable to the public in the way that the administration now holds itself out to be — and as articulated explicitly in the accountability system for principal officials.

Does the system deliver the right policies?

Hong Kong appears, therefore, to operate a policy-making system which is, on the one hand, overweight with the influence of the tycoonocracy, while being capable, on the other hand, of being swayed by pockets of public opinion, even if emanating only from a minority. These processes are a poor substitute for proper democratic procedures and democratic accountability, which Hong Kong lacks.

Despite those shortcomings, the fact remains that, as noted in Chapter 1, Hong Kong's economy has, taking one year with the next, been performing pretty well. During the late 1990s it was hit by the Asian crisis of 1997, the collapse of the local property bubble, the Hong Kong dollar crisis of 1998, the onset of five years of price deflation, and the SARS crisis. This caused many in Hong Kong, including notably the chief executive, to lose, or give the impression of losing, confidence in the economy's longer-term prospects. There was many a doleful speech from the chief executive about the challenge of restructuring, and a hint of desperation in negotiations with the Mainland for the privileges of CEPA. The reality, however, is that, after occasional years of recession, the economy is now flourishing, and self-confidence has returned. This is despite the fact that indecision and compromise have become more apparent in the execution of economic policy, as in the case of the west Kowloon cultural hub, redevelopment of the Tamar and Kai Tak sites, the future development of Lantau, the problem of traffic congestion related to non-optimal tunnel tolls, delays over consultation for the goods and services tax, delayed decisions over new railway routes, and so on.

Under pressure from vested interests, the government sometimes appears to lose sight of the fact that the essentials which make an economy competitive lie on the supply side — a well qualified, flexible and entrepreneurial labour force, a business-friendly environment, and so on. It should not concentrate unduly on trying to predict which sectors will face the strongest demand and then tailoring policy specifically to those sectors. That is a task for the private sector itself. Resources will naturally be drawn to the strongest. If government tries to second-guess, it may end up with costly mistakes — like Cyberport. Meanwhile, those sectors in which Hong Kong has clearly possessed a comparative advantage, such as finance and business services, do not anyway need government support.

In sum, the nature of the policy-making process is flawed on two scores. First, it is overweight with business interests. Economic policy itself has become too dirigiste, both in response to those sectional interests and because government became scared during the recession years into believing that it ought to be more proactive in steering the economy. Second, the policy makers have too often been scared off by fear of adverse popular reaction.

As regards conscious intervention, the Basic Law reads as though it is more permissive towards intervention in the economy than it is towards budgetary flexibility. The economy has generally performed well, but without some of the government's tinkering it might have done better still. The government would probably do better to limit its interventions to improving the supply side.

Conclusions

As China re-emerged from political and economic isolation in the final quarter of the twentieth century, so Hong Kong re-emerged as the dominant entrepot trading and business centre for China. Hong Kong is now being swept along by China's rapid growth. It may no longer possess the quasi-monopolistic advantages that it once enjoyed, when it was virtually the only gateway to China and provided a range of services for China which China was not yet in a position to provide for itself. Nowadays Hong Kong has to compete much more for its business, not least against Mainland cities. But compete it does, and very effectively. Too often the burgeoning strength of the Mainland economy is seen as a threat, whereas in fact it is Hong Kong's lifeblood and a huge opportunity. The challenge for Hong Kong is to retain its competitive attraction through the sensible execution of macroeconomic policies, and through careful attention to maintaining the attractive supply-side environment which has facilitated its dynamism over past decades.

Indeed, success would not have come to Hong Kong, historically, had not successive administrations nurtured an inviting and reasonably stable business climate. Hong Kong was once caricatured as a hotbed of unbridled capitalism. That was always something of an exaggeration, and the more so today when Hong Kong prides itself in matching the broad sweep of legal and regulatory standards expected of an advanced economy. But the government nevertheless boasts that it keeps intervention in the economy to the minimum that is strictly necessary.

Believing that minimal intervention is the best formula for both maintaining a strong economy and attracting international business, the government works hard to promote the perception of Hong Kong as a free economy, and shows great delight when ranking lists confirm it. The administration is perhaps overly self-conscious about the rankings and ratings that are conferred upon it by outsiders of all sorts, and too sensitive to criticism. The various surveys tend to confirm that, although Hong Kong may be wanting in certain aspects of quality of life, it is indeed regarded as a good place to do business, partly because of its reputation for hands-off government.

However, this hands-off image turns out to be something of an illusion. The discussion in Chapter 3 revealed that the government has, over the years, been quite heavily involved in directing or influencing, with varying degrees of success, the type of economic activity carried out in Hong Kong. Meanwhile, its much vaunted budgetary discipline is not as tight as it appears to be at first sight, principally because of give-aways of land which do not feature in the accounts. Moreover, the budget is subject to a confusing set of rules and conventions, both formal and informal, which almost certainly distort resource allocation, and consequently cause economic inefficiency. Only in the realm of monetary policy is the administration seen to maintain a sufficient degree of detachment to give full credence to the non-interventionist label. Meanwhile, in dogged defence of non-interventionism, the government for many years sought to make a virtue of minimal intervention to counteract monopolistic practices, despite this being one area which was crying out for actual intervention — a point which government now appears to have conceded.

In Chapter 3, interventionist leanings were traced back to the 1970s, paradoxically a period when the most ardent exponent of non-intervention was serving as financial secretary. From the late 1980s until the handover of sovereignty in 1997, the urge to intervene may have tailed off, most likely because the economy was faring well, partly due to the catalytic effect of a resurgent Mainland. However, after the handover, whether because of the various adverse shocks which hit the economy over the ensuing few years, causing recession and deflation, or because of the latitude seemingly offered by the Basic Law, or simply because Chief Executive Tung Chee Hwa desired to be seen as a proactive leader, interference in the economy appeared to move up a gear. There is a long list of measures and desiderata that he pronounced upon, from the grandiose and expensive to the nigh-trivial and cheap, spreading across virtually every sector.

Donald Tsang, since he took over as chief executive, and his financial secretary Henry Tang, have displayed less interventionist tendencies, at least insofar as there have been no major new initiatives and there has been evident restraint from handing little parcels of assistance to all and sundry. Against that, however, one might flag two notable developments: the reference to Hong Kong in the Mainland's five-year plan (plus Tsang's enthusiastic response to it), and Tsang's relaunch of the Commission on Strategic Development. Both, by their very terminology, conjure up visions of a greater degree of dirigisme in economic policy than would seem appropriate to Hong Kong's *laissez-faire* aspirations. However, neither has, thus far, led to any significant shift of policies in that direction. Even so, they establish a planning framework, and vigilance may be needed to ensure that the output from their processes continues to focus on improving the supply-side of the economy, and the business and social environment, rather than on specific interventions to shape sectoral activity.

That vigilance is necessary because the Hong Kong government does not always appear to have fully appreciated the distinction between policies which — to use its own words — facilitate and those which lead. A government truly committed to a market economy might have been expected to place relatively more emphasis than the Hong Kong government has on the supply side (in matters such as training and education, for example). This is not to deny that the government does indeed take such things seriously and provides considerable resources for them, but a reading of policy addresses and budget speeches, certainly during the years when Tung Chee Hwa was running Hong Kong, suggests that the main focus of policy was on picking winners, rather than on simply providing the environment in which the winners would self-select.

Whatever policies may have emerged, whether on the supply side, or the more contentious ones such as those in support of financial concessions for particular sectors or in favour of persevering with a strategy of high land prices, they must have originated from somewhere. But where? Part III surveyed the institutional framework and the possible channels of influence on policy. It reached the conclusion that the entire process was, not unexpectedly, somewhat amorphous. A worrying feature is that there does not appear to have been any mechanism for subjecting policies to a rigorous intellectual appraisal before they run too far, in order to ensure not only that they satisfy proximate criteria (such as cost-benefit analysis in the case of project spending), but also that they are consistent with broader strategic objectives.

Thus, to take a recent example, if it is proposed to grant land at a concessionary price for a logistics park on Lantau Island, a disinterested party should be required to review objectively whatever social cost-benefit analysis has been carried out by the advocates, to address the question of why a subsidy is needed for an essentially commercial venture, and to assess how such a subsidy would fit in with the government's overarching non-interventionist philosophy. The official studies, referred to in Chapter 3, did not deal substantively with those points.

By way of another example, one might consider the administration's stance on competition policy. For years it argued against a general pro-competition law, maintaining that its case-by-case sectoral approach was sufficient to deal with any problems. Now it has changed its tune and accepted (or so it seems — the process is not yet complete) the case for legislating. What has brought about that change of heart? There has not been any notable change in prevailing competitive or anti-competitive conditions across the economy. But, earlier, the IMF and, more recently, the government-appointed review body have produced analysis and intellectual arguments in favour of a new law. Yet the basic facts and arguments have been around for years. The government was doubtless aware of them, but maintained its obstinate stance, in the belief that this accorded with its *laissez-faire* credo. Whether it now accepts that it was mistaken, or is simply caving in to international opinion and popular pressure, is unclear. This episode shows a certain shallowness in strategic thinking.

The regrettable fact is that, despite the existence of the Central Policy Unit and the Commission on Strategic Development, intellectual leadership has been weak, hiding behind the veneer of mere slogans such as 'the market leads, government facilitates'. There is no sign of a coherent intellectual framework or strategic blueprint against which policies can be tested. This is as relevant when considering the nexus of fiscal rules, the pricing of land, housing policy and possible new taxes, as it is when dealing with questions of support for particular producing sectors of the economy. Rather, the impression is given of an endless process of *ad hoc* assessments. Given this situation, it has not been difficult for business interests to insinuate their ideas into the policy process, as discussed in Chapter 8.

At the same time, however, because the government continues to lack a comprehensive democratic mandate, and because of the known wish of the Mainland authorities that Hong Kong should remain tranquil, the government has some difficulty in introducing any policies which cannot command the widest consensus. Paradoxically, an executive-led government with, on paper, quite extensive powers is frequently finding itself struck with a sort of paralysis.

Need one worry about the influence of business? After all, it has long been held that 'what is good for business must be good for Hong Kong' — a view which can draw support from the economy's enviable long-term performance. The answer to that question comes in three parts.

First, there is no way of knowing how the economy would have performed under some different set of circumstances, such as with less sectoral aid, fewer government efforts to support manufacturing or new technologies, and a budgetary system less dependent on land premiums, less skewed towards capital projects or more geared towards income redistribution.

However, secondly, one could be fairly certain that dilution or banishment of the business elite from the corridors of power would lead to a change in the mindset of the administration. It might be spared much of the special pleading — and hence the pressure to provide direct or indirect support for particular sectors. It might feel freer to indulge in some blue-skies thinking about land supply and prices. It might feel less inhibited about increasing social and welfare provision, or extracting higher tax revenue from those most able to pay. It might find it easier to tackle some of the more egregious economic scandals, such as the power companies' guaranteed monopoly profits. All in all, the process of running the economy would become more objective and be freer of the influence of vested interests. That ought to result in better policies and an improved allocation of economic resources.

Thirdly, there is a socio-political angle. The gulf between rich and poor is wide and probably widening. Although there has been no major confrontation on this issue, the public is becoming more politically aware and increasingly willing to voice its opinions, and Legislative Council members are ready speak out on all manner of issues. Political parties and think-tanks, though they may not have made huge contributions in the past, can be expected to provide an ever-increasing dimension to public debate, despite any present feeling of impotence and exasperation at the policy-making process as it currently functions. The longer that the unholy alliance between government and business persists, which is seen by many as one of the obstacles to more redistribution of prosperity, the greater are likely to be the tensions which build up and which could lead to the sort of public expressions of dissatisfaction which the government is so keen to avoid. The government's formation of the Commission on Poverty may have defused the issue for the short term. But unless the commission produces some substantive proposals to alleviate poverty, recriminations against the elite of society and their presumed political influence may intensify. The era of quiet deference is past.

Whatever the precise influence of different groups in the policy process may be, this book has found that the government in Hong Kong has for many years been practising a rather more hands-on approach to economic policy than its own propaganda would have one believe. That itself might not matter much, if one could be confident that the policy decisions were founded on sound, thorough and objective economic analysis, within a clear and consistent strategic framework. Sadly, those conditions are seldom satisfied. Intellectual leadership is lacking. Vested interests from the business world have always been influential, but have been more so since the end of British rule. Meanwhile, because of the absence of full democracy, the government is too often frightened off by populist opposition from proceeding with its preferred policies. Regrettably, the good policies are just as likely to suffer that fate as are the bad.

Despite all the shortcomings in the nature and process of economic policy which have been identified in this book, the Hong Kong economy generally flourishes, and continues to be the envy of much of the rest of the world. Nevertheless, a number of the problems which have been identified, such as weakness in the intellectual foundation of budget strategy and the growing paralysis of the overall policy-making process, are ones which will, if not actively addressed, persist. And if they are allowed to persist, they could result in significant under-performance of the economy. The administration should put more effort into tackling these fundamental issues, even if that means spending less time on grandiose, wide-ranging action agendas, of the sort which were spawned in response to the mention of Hong Kong in the Mainland's five-year plan.

Notes

1   Government press release, 8 September 2005.
2   Government press release, 29 September 2005.
3   HKMA *Annual Report* 2004.
4   Government press release, 26 September 2005. It may be noted, in passing, that overdependence on being in the rating agencies' good books may predispose economic policies towards conservatism; this could result, for example, in severe fiscal restraint and accumulation of massive foreign exchange reserves, neither of which, though pleasing to the financial markets, would necessarily accord with optimal economic policies.
5   Government press releases, 18 April 2006 and 27 July 2006.
6   IMF Staff Report on Article IV consultations with Hong Kong, May 2003.
7   Competition policy is covered in more detail in Chapter 6.
8   Government press release, 14 February 2006.
9   "Six-monthly report on Hong Kong, January–June 2004", July 2004, Cm 6292.
10 As recorded by Leo Goodstadt in *Uneasy Partners: The Conflict between Public Interest and Private Profit in Hong Kong* (Hong Kong: Hong Kong University Press, 2005, p. 121), quoting in turn from David Lethbridge (ed.), *The Business Environment in Hong Kong* (Hong Kong: Oxford University Press, 1980), p. xii.
11 Leo Goodstadt, *Uneasy Partners*, quoting from *Hong Kong Hansard*, 26 February 1986.
12 These points are discussed in greater detail by Leo Goodstadt, *Uneasy Partners*. Drawing on *One Country, Two Systems. An Account of the Drafting of the Hong Kong Basic Law* by Xiao Weiyun (Beijing: Peking University Press 2001, pp. 419–22), he suggests that the "plain intention of the Basic Law's drafters was that the post-colonial administration should be involved more extensively in economic management than its British predecessor".
13 Quotations taken from a report in the *South China Morning Post,* 25 January 2005.
14 As depicted by Donald Tsang, the then financial secretary, during a speech in Boston, 14 June 2000.

15 Information note by the Government Secretariat for the Legislative Council, October 1999.

16 Government press release, 8 July 2005.

17 The Hong Kong Jockey Club is the body which runs horse-racing in Hong Kong and has a monopoly on all forms of gambling (e.g. horse-racing, soccer, and the weekly 'mark six' lottery). Its profits, after payment of betting duty to the government, are spent on charitable projects in the spheres of education, medical care, sports and recreation, community services, etc.

18 The government's director of audit, in his report no. 48 of March 2007, criticised the ASTRI for over-generous staff pay and expenses, and for deficiencies in project planning and monitoring. He also queried expenditure on fung shui consultants.

19 Richard Wong and Alan Siu, "Reviving Hong Kong's competitiveness", Hong Kong Institute of Economics and Business Strategy, April 2004.

20 The reference to the supply side deserves some elaboration. It has never been intended that the concept of non-interventionism should proscribe policies aimed at freeing up markets (of which the Closer Economic Partnership Arrangement is a particularly relevant example), raising educational standards, providing public infrastructure, ensuring necessary (but not excessive) regulation, and so forth. These may broadly be termed 'supply-side' measures, as distinct from attempts to manage aggregate demand or interventions directed at particular industries or sectors.

21 Proceedings of the Legislative Council (*Hansard*), 1 June 2005, columns 7970–71.

22 Government press release, 18 May 2006.

23 Chief executive's address to the summit; government press release, 11 September 2006.

24 See *Report on Economic Summit on "China's 11th Five-Year Plan and the Development of Hong Kong"*, accessible at www.info.gov.hk/info/econ_summit/eng/action.html.

25 Thus far, the Mainland authorities have been commendably 'hands-off'. A notable exception has occurred in financial policy, where the Mainland has, in effect, dictated the pace of development of renminbi banking business in Hong Kong, even though banks in Hong Kong are in principle free to develop foreign currency business as they wish, subject only to the constraints of prudent banking.

26 Budget speech, 6 March 2002.

27 In this context 'recurrent' is synonymous with 'current' (as opposed to 'capital'); the recurrent balance is also commonly referred to in Hong Kong as the 'operating' balance.

28 Unless the architects of the Basic Law intended that the Hong Kong government should count borrowing as revenue, as it has been doing in its accounts. But this is a highly eccentric practice, which would not be recognised as best accounting practice, and which contradicts agreed international standards for government accounts laid down by the International Monetary Fund.

29 With the exception of the site of St John's Anglican Cathedral, which is held as freehold.

30 Information Note, "Land supply in Hong Kong", *Legislative Council Secretariat,* IN20/05–06.

31 Statement on housing policy, 2002.

32 See, for example, Richard Y. C. Wong, "Public housing reform and its effects on the private housing market", HKCER Letters, Vol. 71 July/August 2002, and James Lee and Lawrence Lau, "Restructuring housing assistance: Benefits for housing, budget and economy", www.hongkongbetter.com.

33 "Broadening the tax base; ensuring our future prosperity".

34 For a fuller historical account, see Tony Latter, "Hong Kong's exchange rate regimes in the twentieth century: The story of three regime changes", Hong Kong Institute for Monetary Research working paper no. 17, 2004, www.hkimr.org.hk.

35 If sterling notes were used in the colony, they had to be bought from the Issue Department of the Bank of England with funds which could then be invested by the Bank of England, on behalf of the British government, to earn it a profit. When a colony issued its own notes, the local colonial administration could itself earn a profit from the sterling investments which it held as backing.

36 In fact, the proportion has persistently exceeded 5%. It was above 11% at the end of 2006. Of course, because of movements in the stock market, a target for equity holdings cannot be met precisely.

37 Details about the history and operation of the Tracker Fund can be found at www.trahk.com.

38 The official stance has shifted somewhat over the years. In January 2000, the chief executive of the Monetary Authority, Joseph Yam, wrote thus "for the time being the answer I am inclined to give to the question of how much foreign reserves we need is 'the more the better'." At that time Hong Kong had the fourth largest reserves of any economy in the world, having been third in 1997. In June 2006, as Hong Kong slipped from seventh to eighth position in that ranking, he admitted: "The build-up of official foreign reserves is not necessarily a good thing, despite the comfort of having more ammunition in the monetary armoury." Both quotations are from Joseph Yam's weekly 'Viewpoint' column, viewable at www.hkma.hk.

39 For an official account of these events, see "Operation of monetary policy" and "Why we intervened", HKMA *Quarterly Bulletin,* November 1998.

40 For a detailed discussion of operational intervention, see Tony Latter, "Rules versus discretion in managing the Hong Kong dollar, 1983–2006", Hong Kong Institute for Monetary Research working paper no. 2, 2007, www.hkimr.org.

41 See www.edlb.gov.hk/edb/eng/resp/psoc.htm.

42 Details of some of these initiatives and complaints are published in the annual reports of the Competition Policy Advisory Group (COMPAG), available at www.compag.gov.hk.

43 "Competition policy: The key to Hong Kong's future economic success", Consumer Council, November 1996.

44 Singapore and China are not, however, without critics of their measures. For example, Singapore has excluded from the law's coverage a swathe of utilities and transport services, largely provided by the public sector. Similarly, China's legislation (though still not finalised at the time of writing), seems set not to tackle administrative monopolies, provincial and municipal barriers to competition, etc. It is feared that it may be aimed more at challenging the strong market positions of foreign companies, than promoting competition across the whole economy.

45 "Promoting competition – maintaining our economic drive", available at www.edlb.gov.hk.

46 Article 45 and Annex I.

47 Legislative Council paper, "Accountability system for principal officials", April 2002.

48 Ibid.

49 Ibid.

50 Prior to the creation of the class of principal officials, the chief executive and the three most senior civil servants were the only 'officials' on the Executive Council.

51 Articles 49 and 50.

52 The 30 functional constituencies are as follows: commerce (2 seats); industry (2 seats); finance; accountancy; labour (3 seats); social welfare; medical; health services; education; legal; engineering; real estate and construction; architecture, surveying and planning; financial services; tourism; district councils; Heung Yee Kuk (new territories village organisation); textiles and garment; import and export; wholesale and retail; transport; information technology; insurance; agriculture and fisheries; sports, performing arts, culture and publication; catering.

53 If a motion, initiated by at least a quarter of the councillors, charges the chief executive with serious breach of law or dereliction of duty and if he or she refuses to resign, the council may, after passing a motion for investigation, give a mandate to the chief justice of the Court of Final Appeal to form and chair an independent investigation committee. The committee shall be responsible for carrying out the investigation and reporting its findings to the council. If the committee considers the evidence sufficient to substantiate such charges, the council may pass a motion of impeachment by a two-thirds majority of all its members and report it to the Central People's Government for decision.

54 See *Functional Constituencies*, edited by Christine Loh and Civic Exchange (Hong Kong: Hong Kong University Press, 2006), Chapter 8.

55 Quotation from the party's policy platform at www.dphk.org.

56 Quotation from the chapter, "Achieving an affluent economy", in the DAB policy platform, accessible at www.dab.org.hk.

57 www.liberal.org.hk.

58 www.cpu.gov.hk.

59 Policy address 2005.

60 *Hong Kong Yearbook 2002;* the figures of 6,000 and 500 refer to executive statutory bodies, such as the Housing Authority and Hospital Authority, as well as to the network of advisory committees. *Hong Kong Yearbook 2005* states that "over 4,000 members of the public are serving on about 400 [advisory and statutory] bodies".

61 Comprehensive data on the degree of disclosure via websites was provided in reply to a Legislative Council question on 18 May 2005 — see official record of proceedings. More recently, the *South China Morning Post* reported (22 February 2007) that, in a survey of some 400 advisory committees, only 67 opened their meetings to the public and only 70 posted substantive documents on the internet.

62 The list is reproduced from the official summary of the commission's first meeting on 25 November 2005.

63 Paper for the February 2006 meeting, www.cpu.gov.hk/english/documents/csd/csd_ec_1_2006.pdf.

64 Government press release, 27 January 2005.

65 www.hkdf.org

66 www.bpf.org.hk

67 www.hkpri.org.hk

68 www.betterhongkong.org

69 www.sepi.org

70 www.civic-exchange.org

71 www.lionrockinstitute.org

72 www.synergynet.org

73 www.bauhinia.org

Index